Milky Way Farms

-

The Way It Was

This is dedicated to my children, Sean and Courtney. Don't let the history of Milky Way Farms fade away and keep all this information intact for future generations. This original information is priceless.

To Franklin C. and Ethel Veronica Mars: Thank you for arriving in Giles County in the bleakest time of our economic history and offering a glimmer of hope that things would be alright.

To the reader of this work: I could have written this as an historical novel, but I chose instead to write it as a purely historical work. Authors can take a little bit of factual information and using what is known as "poetic license" make the story turn out the way they want it to. This work could have been much, much longer if I had chosen to take that route. I have used pictures and letters from my Milky Way Farms material to show the reader that what they are reading is factual and portrays events as they actually unfolded, rather than the way I would have had them take place. Some articles and advertisements in this work appeared in the Pulaski Citizen newspaper and are used with the permission of the Pulaski Citizen. The author is greatly appreciative of this permission.

God blessed me to be able to share this information with you. I hope you enjoy this look into the history of "Milky Way Farms."

I couldn't start to tell this story without first telling you about the man that made my ability to tell it happen. Sam T. Collins Jr. was born February 3, 1912 in Campbellsville, Tennessee. Campbellsville High School had a very good football team the four years while he was in high school. No, don't get me wrong, it wasn't just because he was on the team. There were a number of outstanding players in those four years. At the end of his senior year he was offered a scholarship to play football at Middle Tennessee State Teachers College.

He went off to school that fall and played on the 1929 team with another young man from Giles County, Smith Howard. Smith Howard played four years, gained a degree and returned to Giles County and became a prominent figure in the field of education. However, my father decided that it would be better if he graduated in one semester and returned to Giles County to pursue who knows what. At any rate, Murfreesboro was a long way from Campbellsville and also a long way from the love of his life, that being my mother. Of course she wasn't my mother yet, that would come later.

When my father returned to Giles County, it was a trying time for everyone. "THE DEPRESSION." He got a job at Reeves Drug Store on the Pulaski square and worked there until they started hiring at Milky Way Farms. This was 1931 and he started at the farm as an assistant bookkeeper. As time progressed he was made the bookkeeper, the assistant farm manager, the farm manager and eventually the resident agent for Mars Incorporated. In May of 1945 the farm was sold to Albert Noe Jr.

When Mr. Noe took over the operation of the farm, my father was asked to stay on as the farm manager until Mr. Noe learned the pitfalls of the management of the farm. When Mr. Noe took over, my father asked him what he wanted to do with all the records and pictures that were located in the office. He told him he could do whatever he wanted with them. My father asked him if he could have them and he said of course. Before the sale of the farm, Mrs. Mars had given my father some of the most personal articles mentioned in this work. These records and pictures were stored for safe keeping for many years. I have told you this so that you will know how I can talk about the technical aspects of the farms operation, the people that were employed and the day-to-day operations of the farm. Not only was I born in the first house to the left of the farm office, but I learned of the farm history through my family's involvement as I grew up.

The farm records and original pictures are the most valuable assets anyone could have in researching the history of Milky Way Farms. To say that I am fortunate to be in possession of this material would be an understatement. Like all people, my father had his faults, but he was a meticulous bookkeeper. If you ever wrote him a letter, he kept that letter and a carbon copy of his response. I have put that correspondence in reverse chronological order so that if you are interested you can read what took place on a daily basis and gain an inside knowledge to the operation of Milky Way Farms.

My father was there from the beginning to after the literal end. My mother always told us that the best years of her life were spent at Milky Way Farms. After we had left the farm and moved to Pulaski, we would sometimes travel north on Highway 31 and my mother would look the other way when we would pass Milky Way Farms. She said that she couldn't bear to see the farm in disarray. A most important piece of Giles County history was gone. That was sad! More about my father later. Now let's continue the story.

Sam T. Collins Jr. in front of the new clubhouse in 1934.

Franklin Clarence Mars was born September 24, 1883 and died April 8, 1934. Mr. Mars had two children, Forrest and Patricia. Forrest became famous in the candy circles and was a driving force in the operation of the company. Patricia married Alan Feeney and together they added to the fame of the farm with the addition of Horned Hereford cattle. The Mars started their candy company in Tacoma Washington known as the Mars Candy Factory. They relocated the factory to Minnesota under the name Mar-O-Bar. The company moved a second time to Chicago and changed the name to Mars Incorporated and the rest is history. Enough about their history and let's continue the story of the farm.

Franklin Clarence Mars.

Ethel Veronica Mars.

Mr. and Mrs. Mars had an associate in the packaging business in Chicago named Eric Schueler. Mr. Schueler's company made boxes for Mars Inc.

These are boxes used by Mars Inc. produced by Eric Schueler's company.

He and his wife invited the Mars to make a trip with them to Pulaski in the spring of 1930. Eric Schueler's wife was from Pulaski and Mr. Schueler had an estate in northern Giles County called Douglas Manor. Mrs. Schueler was the daughter of Senator C.C. Brown. While Mr. and Mrs. Mars were in Giles County they were struck with the beauty of the county and decided they wanted to build a show place estate just north of Pulaski on Richland Creek on both sides of the "bee-line" highway, now known as U.S. 31 highway.

Mr. Mars patterned Milky Way Farms after a famous estate in Chazy, New York named Heart's Delight Farm. Heart's Delight Farm was comprised of eleven thousand acres and was located in Champlain Valley, 183 miles north of Albany and 50 miles south of Montreal. Heart's Delight was devoted to raising pure bred horses, Shorthorn and Holstein-Friesian cattle, Dorset and Southdown sheep, Chester white and Yorkshire swine, white leghorn chickens, turkeys and pigeons. A copy of the Heart's Delight Farm catalog and visitors brochure is located in my collection of information. As this story unfolds you will be able to see the likeness between Milky Way Farms and Heart's Delight.

Heart's Delight Farm Brochure.

Milky Way Farms was acquired from January 1931 until mid-1933. Sixteen separate tracts that totaled 2805 acres were purchased for $172,792.00 or $61.60 per acre. Remember this was early on in the depression and there were mixed emotions about this rich man from up north coming to Giles County and buying land. Don't get me wrong, the land owners that needed to either sell their land or lose it were glad to see Frank Mars. One thing that made Frank Mars rather distasteful was the fact that he was a "Republican". At that time, and up until recently Giles County was a staunch democratic stronghold. Most people wouldn't even admit that they knew a republican.

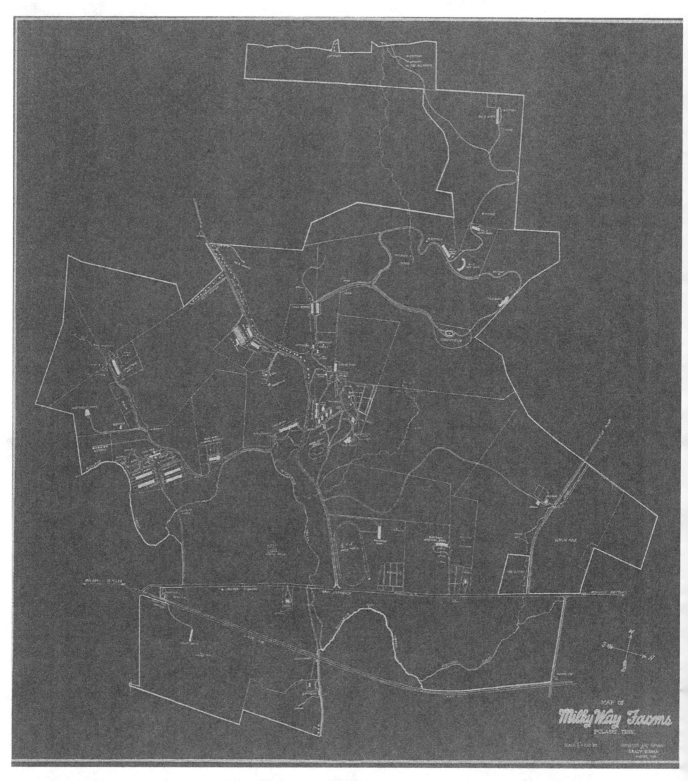

This map was actually made in 1937 and it doesn't fit in chronological order here but it will be a good place to show it so that you can get an idea of size of the entire farm.

Milky Way Reo trucks had advertisements for Herbert Hoover.

The merchants and bankers in Giles County were very appreciative that Mr. Mars was here. Evidence this article in the Pulaski Citizen.

The Pulaski Citizen, January 7, 1931. "The Citizen on behalf of Giles County extends a cordial greeting and hearty welcome to Mr. F.C. Mars, wealthy candy manufacturer, and saddle-horse fancier of Chicago who closed a deal Saturday for a tract of land which when plans are carried through is destined in the near future to become one of the most attractive estates and show places of Middle Tennessee.

MILKY WAY FARMS CLUB HOUSE

Congratulations

: TO THE :

CITIZEN

: ON ITS :

82nd BIRTHDAY

Congratulations

: TO THE :

CITIZEN

: ON ITS :

82nd BIRTHDAY

: FROM :

Tennessee's Home

: OF :

Pure Bred Livestock

Milky Way Farms

MIDDLE TENNESSEE
O PULASKI, TENN

Both this ad out of the newspaper and the previous ad show how Milky Way Farms was glad to be in Giles County just as this article where I have inserted these ads talks about how Giles County is thankful that they were here.

The plentiful water from natural springs was important at Milky Way Farms.

Mr. Mars has a stable of fancy saddle horses, now located in California. But California is a long way from Chicago where his business is located. About a month ago he came to Pulaski for a visit with his friend Eric Schueler. And while here became impressed with our hills, and springs, and blue grass pastures. Some of our citizens, among them S.H. Woodard took an interest in showing the visitor about, and answering his questions as to climate, rainfall, temperatures, summer and winter, etc.

The result of it all was that Saturday a deal was closed whereby Mr. Mars became the owner of a tract of land comprising nearly six hundred acres, where the Bee Line Highway crosses Richland Creek for a consideration of about $50,000 cash. The estate was cut from the Tacker-Woodard farm and of the Rhea lands, from about three quarters of a mile on the west side of the Bee-Line highway and extends westward down Richland Creek Valley about a mile and a half, including some hills and four good springs which flow southward to the creek. The estate lies on both sides of Richland Creek, but the greater part of it is north and west of the creek.

As soon as the deal was closed, Mr. Mars and his architect, Jack Drake, who will be in charge and supervise improvements for a year began to give orders in a way to almost make our conservative people dizzy.

The first order was for 100,000 feet of lumber, delivery to start within a week. Work has already started on a roadway from the highway. Two cars of cement were ordered for use in concrete foundations. And Mr. Drake expects to have about thirty-five carpenters on the job by next Monday.

Every building and every scrap of wire fencing are to be removed, and new buildings of harmonious design are to be erected. Board fencing painted white will enclose the estate and paddocks.

The first building to be erected is horse barn, sixty by three hundred feet, and if conditions are favorable it is expected to have this ready early in February. Mr. Mars desires to ship his horses from California about the first of February and wants the new barn ready to take of them on arrival here."

ANNOUNCEMENT

Milky Way Farm

We have installed one of the Fairbank-Morse Register Type Scales and we will be ready to receive ear corn on

Friday, November 6th

Price to be $1.60 per barrel delivered. 44-45

Not only did Milky Way Farms want to bring horses soon but they also wanted corn and oats delivered for feed and let the people know that they had the most modern scales so that they would be treated fairly.

Mr. Mars' favorite horse was one of the first to arrive at the farm.

Sept. 4, 1940

Mr. F. E. Mars
C/O A. A. Meyer
126 Gale Avenue
River Forest, Illinois.

Dear Mr. Mars:

I am sorry to advise that your gray horse passed away
yesterday. The boys found him sick in the paddock yesterday
morning about 10:30 O'Clock and we called Dr. J. W. Berry,
Veterinarian in Pulaski immediately. He diagnosed the case
as a twisted intestine when he came. The horse passed away
about 1:30 O'Clock yesterday afternoon. Dr. Berry performed
a post mortem immediately after death and he said the cause
of death was a twisted intestine and ruptured stomach.
I watched the post mortem and his intestines were twisted
and his stomach ruptured.

I am very sorry that this happened. Alan saw the horse also
and saw his condition before he died. We did everything
possible to save him.

If you had insurance on this horse you can forward the
papers to me and I will have Dr. Berry fill them out for
you.

With kindest regards, I am

Most Sincerely,

This letter is out of chronological order but I wanted to put it near the picture of Mr. Mars' favorite
horse. Forrest Mars has not been discussed much in this work. The one thing he wanted from Milky
Way Farms was his father's horse. Unfortunately, as this letter explains, the horse died before it was
removed to a place provided by Forrest E. Mars.

Another article from the Pulaski Citizen helps explain what was thought to be taking place. "It is said the stable contains one fancy saddle mare for which Mr. Mars paid $25,000 dollars, another that cost $16,000. There are sixteen groomsmen who take care of the horses, in addition to other attendants, and servants about the place. A training track and polo grounds will be laid out and suitable quarters provided for the people.

Mr. Mars expects to build a residence or house later, but will not get to that for several months. Provisions must first be made for the horses and their keepers. Mr. Mars plans to spend approximately $150,000 in improvements within a year or two, in addition to cost of the land.

All electric wiring will be put under ground so no unsightly poles will mar the beauty of the place nor endanger any man or animal in case of accident. And all land not now in grass will be put in pasture as quickly as the grass will grow. Mr. Mars says he can buy all the corn, oats and hay be needs from local farmers so does not have to bother about raising it. He plans to spend all the money he can with Giles County people with whom he comes to locate his hobby. Of course, if our people do not provide what he wants, he will buy elsewhere. Mr. Mars business is making and selling "Milky Way Candy". His diversion is raising some of the best bred fancy saddle horses in the United States. There is always a market for these horses at good prices. No other form of exercise has quite the thrill that goes with riding a well-bred, stylish, nice mannered horse. And this diversion is quite popular especially among people closely confined by office work.

Mr. Mars can leave Chicago by airplane with a party of friends Friday noon, spend the weekend on his estate here which will be called the "Milky Way Farms" and if occasion requires he can be back in Chicago for business Monday morning.

We sincerely hope Mr. Mars and his interesting family may find all they anticipate in climate, soil, water and neighbors and that he may never have occasion to regret his choice of a location for his breeding establishment. And perhaps when friends come to visit him they too will be favorably impressed with the wonderful natural advantages of Giles County and Richland valley. This immediate vicinity was once the home of many famous race horses. And natural advantages are just as good now as they ever were.

The many friends of Rogers Tacker will be interested to learn that he is to be foreman in charge of preparation of the land, sowing grass, and in fact all the work except the building which will be under supervision of Mr. Drake and care of the horses which will be in charge of expert groomsmen."

By the middle of June, 1931 saddle horses were being shipped in and arriving weekly. Seventeen additional saddle horses and geldings were unloaded on June 8, 1931. This shipment increased the number of pure-bred, registered saddle horses at Milky Way Farms to about ninety including some half dozen colts. If you included nineteen work mules that would bring the total number to over a hundred. Keep in mind that Frank Mars liked saddle horses. The race horses will be added later.

Mr. Mars was so interested in being in Giles County that he moved a southern headquarters of Mars Inc. to Nashville so that he could be in close touch with his business. Evidence this article from the Pulaski Citizen of May 20, 1931.

"Nashville, May 18 – Southern headquarters of Mars, Inc., Chicago, manufacturers of Milky Way confectionery, will be established at Nashville at the Bennie-Dillon building it was announced today by W.W. Dillon, Jr.

The sales force of the company will move to Nashville and take over the offices in the local building on June 1, Mr. Dillon stated.

Although no long term lease has been signed on the suite of offices it is the expectation of Frank C. Mars, head of the company to maintain divisional headquarters in Nashville permanently the lessors of the office understand.

The move to Nashville, although it has not been previously announced has been rumored since the purchase by Mr. Mars of the "Milky Way Farm" an extensive estate in Giles County, where he has become engaged in the breeding of show horses.

The volume of work in connection with the improvements in progress at Milky Way Farm is not generally appreciated. Our information is that nearly four hundred people are employed including all classes. And that the payroll for wages and material last week exceeded $12,000. And this work has been in progress since mid-winter."

It is worthy to note that at this time Mrs. Mars name has not been mentioned. You will see that she will become extremely important in the development and building of the Milky Way Farms image.

As noted in the July 22, 1931 edition of the Pulaski Citizen Mr. Mars purchased an additional 116 acres from William O'Neal. This was a good addition to an already fine farm.

By September of 1931 the people of Giles County were extremely happy that Milky Way Farms had given jobs to hundreds of its population. The announcement at this time of the addition of a purebred Hereford cattle herd was evidence to the local population that Mr. Mars was happy with his land purchases and was here to stay. The first group of Herefords numbered ninety cows and heifers as a test. Rogers Tacker went to Kansas City where he wanted to buy about four hundred more young cows. The people of Giles County were glad to hear this since that would mean a larger force of workers would have to be employed to clear land, provide barns, milking, feeding and caring for a large herd of cattle. More good news was on the way when Mr. Mars purchased the Charley Jenkins place of 142 acres immediately adjoining the Milky Way Farms land on the south and the Rainey Cobb farm of 426 acres that joined Jenkins and Milky Way Farms. These two land acquisitions brought the total to more than a thousand acres. The trip to Kansas City by Mr. Tacker did not produce the four hundred head that he had hoped for so he went to Texas to complete his order.

As the farm began to take shape there were ads run in the local paper about the progress of the farm. One announcement in November, 1931 was to let the local farmers know that the farm had installed one of the Fairbank-Morse Register Type Scales and that they would be ready to receive ear corn on Friday, November 6th. The price that would be paid was $1.60 per barrel delivered. It was important for local farmers to know that they had the most modern scales to weigh their products that were delivered to the farm. The farm also advertised for hay. They wanted a limited quantity of clover, bean, pea and oat hay. Clover hay would be bought for ten dollars a ton and bean, pea and oat hay would be bought for eight dollars a ton delivered to the farm. This was very important for local farmers to have a market for what they produced.

To show the appreciation that the local merchants had for Mr. Mars and Milky Way Farms, ads were run in the local paper.

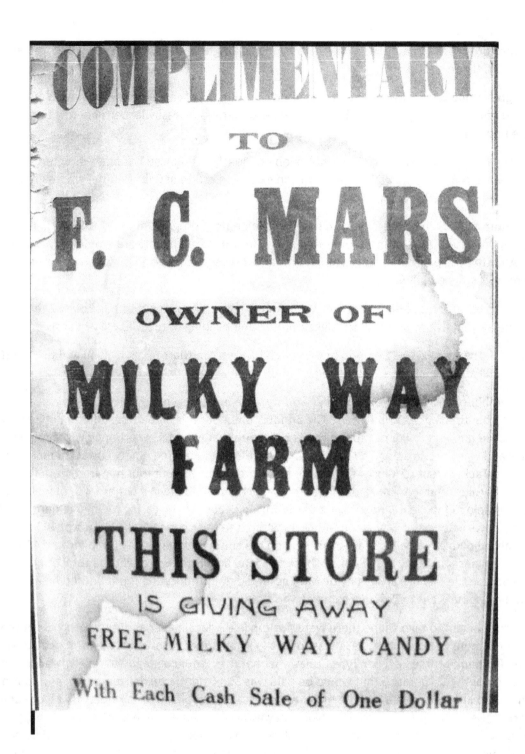

Free candy for Christmas. As a token of appreciation of the service rendered by Mr. F.C. Mars to citizens of Giles County, in giving employment for labor and providing a market for corn, hay and other products, the undersigned merchants, without consulting Mr. Mars have arranged to feature Milky Way candy for the trade week beginning Monday Dec. 7 and continuing through Saturday December 12.

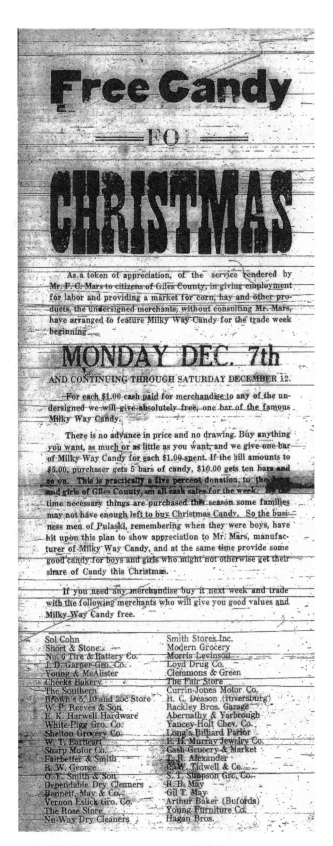

Free Candy

FOR

CHRISTMAS

As a token of appreciation, of the service rendered by Mr. F. C. Mars to citizens of Giles County, in giving employment for labor and providing a market for corn, hay and other products, the undersigned merchants, without consulting Mr. Mars, have arranged to feature Milky Way Candy for the trade week beginning

MONDAY DEC. 7th

AND CONTINUING THROUGH SATURDAY DECEMBER 12.

For each $1.00 cash paid for merchandise to any of the undersigned we will give absolutely free, one bar of the famous Milky Way Candy.

There is no advance in price and no drawing. Buy anything you want, as much or as little as you want, and we give one bar of Milky Way Candy for each $1.00 spent. If the bill amounts to $5.00, purchaser gets 5 bars of candy, $10.00 gets ten bars and so on. This is practically a five percent donation, to the boys and girls of Giles County, on all cash sales for the week. time necessary things are purchased this season some families may not have enough left to buy Christmas Candy. So the business men of Pulaski, remembering when they were boys, have hit upon this plan to show appreciation to Mr. Mars, manufacturer of Milky Way Candy, and at the same time provide some good candy for boys and girls who might not otherwise get their share of Candy this Christmas.

If you need any merchandise buy it next week and trade with the following merchants who will give you good values and Milky Way Candy free.

Sol Cohn	Smith Stores Inc.
Short & Stone	Modern Grocery
No. 6 Tire & Battery Co.	Morris Levinson
J. D. Garner Gro. Co.	Loyd Drug Co.
Young & McAlister	Clemmons & Green
Cheeks Bakery	The Fair Store
The Southern	Currin-Jones Motor Co.
Brown's 5, 10 and 25c Store	H. C. Deason (Hiversburg)
W. P. Reeves & Son	Rackley Bros. Garage
E. K. Harwell Hardware	Abernathy & Yarbrough
White-Pigg Gro. Co.	Yancey-Holt Chev. Co.
Shelton Grocery Co.	Long's Billiard Parlor
W. T. Earheart	E. H. Murray Jewelry Co.
Sharp Motor Co.	Cash Grocery & Market
Fairbetter & Smith	T. R. Alexander
R. W. George	G. W. Tidwell & Co.
O. E. Smith & Son	S. T. Simpson Gro. Co.
Dependable Dry Cleaners	R. B. May
Bennett, May & Co.	Gil T. May
Vernon Eslick Gro. Co.	Arthur Baker (Bufords)
The Rose Store	Young Furniture Co.
Nu-Way Dry Cleaners	Hagan Bros.

This ad as a token of appreciation from the local merchants and business men shows how glad they were that the Mars family had chosen their community to build such a farm.

Another ad in the local paper read: As a token of recognition and appreciation of F.C. Mars maker of famous Milky Way candy who is locating the greatest saddle horse breeding establishment in the world here in Giles County, the Pulaski chamber of commerce, local banks and other citizens donate this valentine advertisement of Milky Way candy.

In the spring of 1932 Mr. Mars closed a deal on 420 acres that joined Milky Way Farms. The J.M. Simmons home place of 240 acres was located on the east side of the highway and south side of Richland Creek. Three lots of the Rheamon land lying on both sides of the highway were also included. This gave Milky Way Farms free access to the creek from both sides. The three lots made up 180 acres. This addition gave the farm approximately 2500 acres on both sides of the creek and the highway. The next land that was acquired was from J. Cayce Abernathy which joined the Rhea lands.

The depression was in full swing and it even had its effect on Mars Inc. In May of 1932 an ad was run in the local paper that told people not to go to the expense of coming out and applying for work.

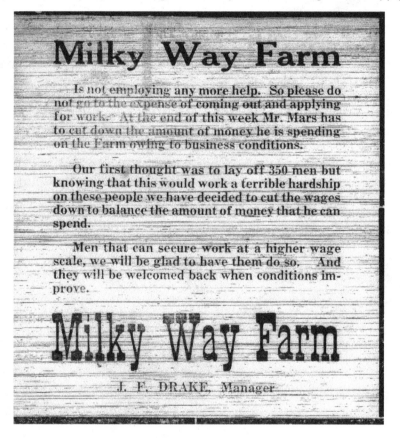

The Pulaski Citizen June 1, 1932: "A distinguished array of national and internationally known livestock men and business men were entertained last week end by Mr. Mars at Milky Way Farms. Assisting Mr. Mars of course in entertaining his guests and providing for their comfort and entertainment were J.F. Drake, Rogers Tacker, Mr. Phillips, Dave Rhea, William O'Neal and others connected with Milky Way Farms.

The guests arrived Saturday morning and were taken by auto for inspection of Milky Way Farms, consisting of 3,000 acres of fertile hills and valleys. They were taken to many high points of vantage where superb views of Milky Way Farms and surrounding countryside could be had. The visitors were all charmed and captivated by the beauty of the entire landscape.

On Saturday afternoon the visitors were treated to a review and inspection of the stock bulls and imported bulls, and many imported bulls from Scotland all of which carry the best blood of the world and constitute the real aristocracy of their kind. They were next carried to the feeding barns where they inspected the commercial cattle which constituted more than 2,500 before spring sales started. The Shorthorn breeding cows and heifers came for review and were the object of great admiration on the part of the visitors. Mr. Mars next took his guests through the horse barns. These barns are works of beauty inside and out. Their architectural designs are beautiful and fit naturally into the landscape. Their hardwood interiors polished to perfection claimed the attention of all. The fine horses housed in these barns completed a perfect picture. The day was ended by an inspection of the stone clubhouse in process of erection, a building whose magnitude and appointments all but stagger the imagination. The day was closed with two boxing bouts on the scene of the old clubhouse. This feature was the real enjoyable event of the day.

Sunday morning the guests gathered at the famous Black place where they talked, smoked and yarned until about 2 o'clock when they were summoned to a high point in a magnificent grove on the Cobb place overlooking Grindstone Hollow, where a delightful lamb barbecue was served in true southern style.

At the conclusion of the barbecue Mr. Wilson was called on by the guests for a talk. He said that he was charmed with Milky Way Farms and with its rare and entrancing beauty. He stated that he had traveled extensively, including Europe and South America and had never seen a spot better suited for the purpose of the building of a great stock farm, pointing out the hills and valleys with their blue grass sod, the springs bursting from every hill and Richland Creek flowing serenely through it all.

Never has so distinguished array of business men been entertained in this county and never were any body of men more simply and perfectly entertained."

Tex McDaniel

You think that variety wasn't the spice of life at Milky Way Farms? This was Tex McDaniel and his trained longhorn. He performed at Milky Way Farms Sep. 8 and 9, 1932.

Mr. Mars was an avid hunter and entertained small groups of friends by taking them bird hunting. He preferred Irish setters as his hunting dog of choice. Bobwhite quail were plentiful in Giles County and were a favorite sport of hunters throughout the county. Before Mr. Mars arrival Irish setters were not primarily used as a dog of choice by the local hunters. Most locals preferred either English setters or pointers.

One of Mr. Mars favorite Irish setters.

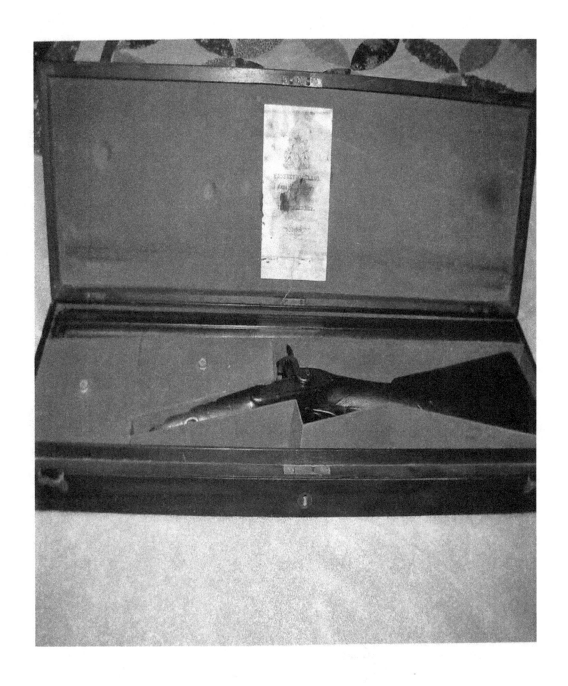

Mr. Mars 1850 model Wesley Richards muzzle loading shotgun.

In 1933 hay was in great demand at Milky Way Farms. The farm wanted to buy local if it could. These ads show what the farm wanted and what they would pay for specified types of hay.

Notice

WE WILL BUY A LIMITED AMOUNT OF HAY AND STRAW AT THE FOLLOWING PRICES:

ALFALFA, TIMOTHY AND CLOVER HAY
PER TON _____ $5.50

PEA, BEAN AND OATS HAY
PER TON _____ $5.00

WHEAT STRAW PER TON _____ $3.50

THESE PRICES ARE F. O. B. YOUR FARM

THIS HAY AND STRAW MUST BE OF GOOD QUALITY AND LOCATED ON ROAD OR HIGHWAY THAT CAN BE TRAVELED BY OUR TRUCKS.

IF INTERESTED IN SELLING GET IN TOUCH WITH US BEFORE OUR REQUIREMENTS ARE FILLED.

Milky Way Farms

PHONE 65

The first clubhouse that has its interior pictured on the next page that you will see in other pictures in this work burned to the ground on Christmas Day of 1931 and was replaced by the clubhouse that is in existence today.

This is an interior angle of the original clubhouse. Do you notice anything a little strange about this?

The September, 1932 Pulaski Citizen had this article about the second clubhouse at Milky Way Farms.

"The handsome clubhouse which has been in course of construction for several months at Milky Way Farms will be completed in January it is said.

This is one of the earliest pictures of the entrance to the farm. If you look closely you can see that the clubhouse is under construction.

This splendid edifice was designed by J.F. Drake, who has been the architect of many buildings belonging to F.C. Mars, in Giles County and other states, and is modeled after the Elizabethan style. Its dimensions are 175 by 45 feet consisting of 26 bedrooms, 13 bathrooms, club room, dining room, smoking room, kitchen, laundry and a complete refrigerating plant is to be installed. The building is two stories high and stone and stucco and timber are being extensively used and tensulate-mineral wood is used for a complete insulating job. The house like all the others on the farms will be lighted with electricity. The hallways are nineteen one half feet wide and a commodious living room is part of the interior ensemble and metal lathing is used throughout.

The stone work was done by John Oman, Jr. who also has the plastering contract. The Standard Company furnished the outfit for the low pressure steam system to be used and also did the plumbing. The National Fire Proof Co's tile will be the roofing used by T.L. Herbert who has the contract.

The clubhouse is located on a well-drained knoll commanding a view of the country for miles around. When completed it will be a model of artistic beauty, combined with modern conveniences and luxurious furnishings and will be as a rich jewel in that rare and costly setting of modern agrarian industry, the Milky Way Farms, of which Giles County is justly proud and Tennessee and the south may well be proud." It might me appropriate at this time to mention that Milky Way Farms was not the only getaway that the Mars family had, they also had a place in Minouqa, Wisconsin known as Marlands.

This example of the construction of the new clubhouse and the barns was a sight to behold. People came from miles around just to observe the building taking place.

How many people at this time in history had a pool like this?

You can see the tennis court in the right behind the diving board.

MARLANDS

From the frozen Northwoods of ice and snow

Where it registers thirty degrees below,

Comes a greeting, friends, of Christmas Cheer,

To wish you a Better and Brighter New Year

Ethel and Frank Mars

Christmas card from Marlands on this and the previous page.

The envelope for the Marlands Christmas Card.

I am pretty sure that I know who this is but I'm not going to identify her since I'm not absolutely sure. All I want to tell you is what I know to be correct. It is a classic picture though, isn't it?

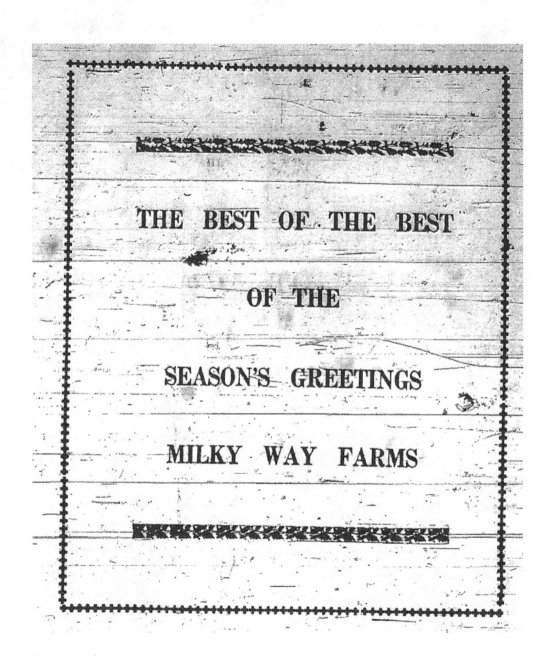

Milky Way Farms expressed its wish for the residents of Giles County to have a merry Christmas.

ENTRANCE TO MIDDLE·TENN·

The latch string is always out-
Nature smiles warmly in her best holiday attire
and beckons you, as we say most heartily.

Merry Christmas
Happy New Year

Milky Way Farms Christmas Card.

Workers installing insulation in the new clubhouse.

The garage below the ice house.

Photo taken as the race track was being built.

The race track under construction.

Social events were held at the farm while the race track was being built. You bet I would like to be able to identify all these people.

Automobiles in front of the office.

As I have already stated, most people believe that Milky Way Farms was devoted to just horned Hereford cattle and race horses. As previously stated the absolute first cattle were shorthorns and the first horses were gaited horses and fine harness or as some people refer to them as road horses. In September 1932 Milky Way Farms made history at the state fair horse show in Nashville. Milky Way Farms entered two mounts in separate events and walked away with two blue ribbons. By winning two first places at the show – the five gaited class and the fine harness class – Milky Way Farms retained its record of winning as many first place ribbons as possible according to the number of horses it had entered at that time. Later in the show the farm had entered eleven horses in nine events and walked away with nine first places and a pair of second place ribbons.

One of the prize winning shorthorn bulls at Milky Way Farms

Jaque Chief, a big chestnut stallion, won the most important event captured by Milky Way Farms. He took the class for five-gaited stallions or geldings and won the right to compete in the grand finals on Saturday night. This horse, one of the best to step on the tanbark, won the five-gaited combined class.

In the fire harness class, Going High, won the five gaited junior class and carried the colors of Milky Way Farms to victory. He was a bay stallion.

John Stewart, the noted handler of horses that Frank Mars put in charge of his horses handled the reins of both winners. Jacque Chief came out easily the winner of the grand championship on the final night.

John Stewart up on Jenette Grey

Road Horse.

A great deal of pride was shown in the beauty and class of show horses at Milky Way Farms. This was taken at a show horse barn at the farm.

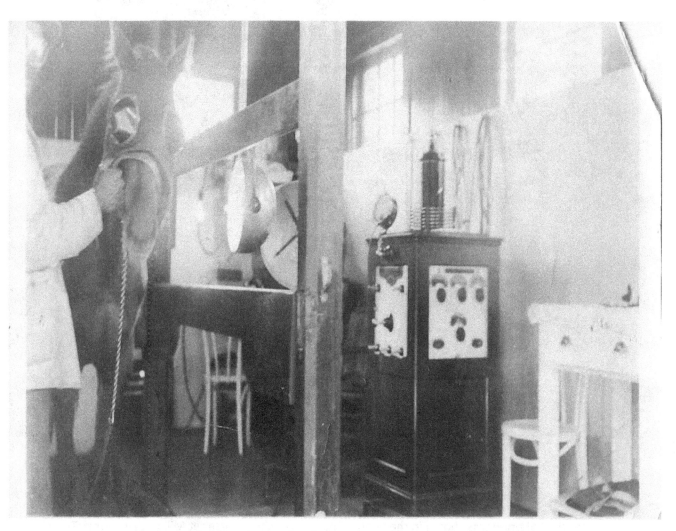

No expense was spared to prep the show horses for the ring. The most modern equipment was used in the show horse barn.

With all the talk about horses and cattle let's not forget that Milky Way Farms was the home of prize winning show mules.

There were mules used every day for all types of work. Tractors existed but were not widespread throughout the south.

IN THE HEART OF THE **NRA** ADVANCING SOUTH

THE MAURY DEMOCRAT

A. B. SOWELL, EDITOR   ESTABLISHED 1882   COVERS MAURY COUNTY

TWELVE PAGES, MINIMUM   COLUMBIA, TENN.   FINE COMMERCIAL PRINTING

August 19, 1933.

Hon S T Collins Jr
MILKY WAY
Pulaski

Dear Mr Collins:-

      Hope you didn't find your car
badly damaged and that it may prove a good
excuse to get a new one - at the other fellow's
expense.   At least, try to hitch-hike to
Columbia Monday night to see "When Ladies Meet".

      I forget to get one of your Milky
Way Chicago envelopes.   Kindly send me one
the size you prefer and I will show you how I can
improve on it.

      Also if you have time, estimate the
amount of straw you have bought in Maury county
this season, as well as the total amount bought
and the price per ton.   Also if you have started
buying hay, the price, quality preferred and
anything else that you may think would be
of interest in the proposed edition.

      Thanking you for the courtesy, as
well as the candy and the order,

      Cordially yours,

      THE MAURY DEMOCRAT

      A B Sowell.

This letter from the Maury Democrat shows how interested the people in Maury County were in what was taking place at Milky Way Farms. The farm had far reaching effects in Middle Tennessee.

After the clubhouse opened Mrs. Mars began to have events and get-to-gathers at the farm. In May of 1933 Mrs. Mars was hostess to an event at the farm as chronicled by the local paper. "Mrs. F.C. Mars was hostess of a very elaborate bridge party Tuesday afternoon entertaining fifty guests at ten tables. A sumptuous repast was served in the banquet hall where place cards were used. There were many handsome prizes and favors given."

TENNESSEE — ISSUED EVERY THURSDAY   THURSDAY, SEPT

(Courtesy Nashvil   Bonner.)

SOCIETY

FERMINE PRIDE - EDITOR
ELEANOR HALL AND FANNY MORAN EZZELL,
ASSOCIATE EDITORS

MRS. FRANK C. MARS, MRS. ERIC SCHUELER,
MISSES HOGAN AND MARS.

Mrs. Frank C. Mars of Chicago and Milky Way Farms, Giles County, with her daughter, Miss Patricia Mars, her niece, Miss Helen Hogan, and her guest, Mrs. Eric Schueler, have been present at the Horse Shows each night of the past week, watching entries from the Milky Way Stables take cups and make splendid showings. Mrs. Mars will remain at her country home for a month before returning to Chicago. Misses Mars and Hogan, who spent the past week at the Hermitage Hotel with Mrs. Mars and Mrs. Schueler, will be boarding students at Ward-Belmont School this year. Mr. and Mrs. Mars were hosts Thursday at Milky Way, entertaining the exhibitors of the Horse Show.

Mrs. Mars, Mrs. Schueler, Patty and Helen Hogan.

When social events were held at the farm they were held at the clubhouse. When the first clubhouse burned all social events were held at the house on the following page. Some people mistakenly believe that this was the first clubhouse but it was actually an existing house on land acquired by the farm. It stood just before you came to Richland Creek going north on Highway 31 on the right side of the highway.

The stone pillars at this entrance are still standing today.

If you were a good basketball player and looking for employment, look no further.

GODWIN DRUG COMPANY
Prescriptions Given Prompt Attention

Drugs, Sundries, Toilet Articles

Cold Drinks, Cigars, Cigarettes Tobaccos

Linden, Tenn., Nov. 7 1933

Mr. S. T. Collins Jr.
Mgr. Basketball Team.
Dear Sir:

I noticed in the paper where you were going to have a basketball team over there on the milky way Farm. What kind of offer can you give a fellow to play with you.

You can ask martin or Clendennin about my playing. I have played against them when they played with Collinwood.

Hoping to hear from you soon.

Yours Truly
Thomas S. Godwin

P.S. Tell me how much I can get a week.

This letter from Thomas Godwin showed the interest in coming to the farm.

Milky Way Farms fielded a basketball team. Their first game was played on Thanksgiving night of 1933 at Martin College. Following the basketball game between Martin College and Union University the spectators were privileged to enjoy the opening game of the season by the newly organized Milky Way Farms team. This team was coached by Dick Wright, former star with the famous Burke Terrors of Nashville. While this team was new some of the players were seasoned veterans. At this time the roster was made up of: Wright, Clendennin, Martin, Rosson, Mann, T. Gordon, Howard, Foster, M.

Collins and A. Gordon. The next team that the Milky Way Farms five entertained was the Y.M.C.A. of Nashville. The Ramblers had some of the best talent in Nashville and was one of Nashville's strong cage teams. The Milky Way Farms – Rambler game was and added attraction at the Martin College gym, Thanksgiving night. A field goal in the last few seconds of play gave the Y.M.C.A. Ramblers a 35 to 33 victory over the Milky Way Farms team. Many members of this team stayed on in Giles County to live and work after the team was disbanded and the farm was sold. I might mention that when World War II began many of the men at the farm were drafted for the war effort. Tommy Gordon, Charlie Martin and Robert Marion (Shorty) Collins are three of those who lived their life in Giles County.

During the Christmas holidays that same year the Milky Way Farms five arranged a schedule which gave promise of some fast ball. All three games were played at the Martin College gym. On Friday night December 22 the game was with the Ideal Aces. On Thursday night December 22 the game was with Burke Terrors and on Saturday night December 30 Cook's Goldbloom came to town. These three teams represented the best independent teams in Nashville

On the previous page is Milky Way's Farms basketball team. Of local interest is Sam Collins, manager; #7 Charlie Martin, #4 Robert M. Collins. Notice the Mars candy on the jerseys.

The logo off the back of a Milky Way Farms warm-up jacket.

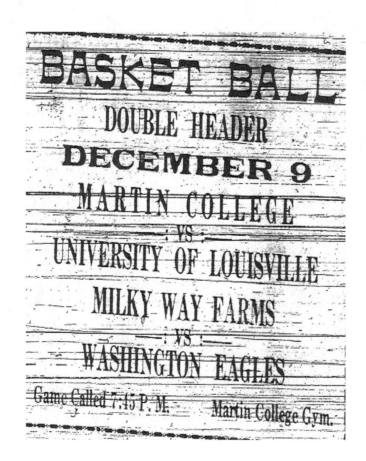

Basket Ball

MARTIN COLLEGE GYM
THURSDAY, JANUARY 4, 1933

MARTIN COLLEGE
: VS :
SALANT AND SALANT
Lawrenceburg

MILKY WAY
VS
SALANT AND SALANT
Boys

Game Called at 7:45   Admission 15c—35c

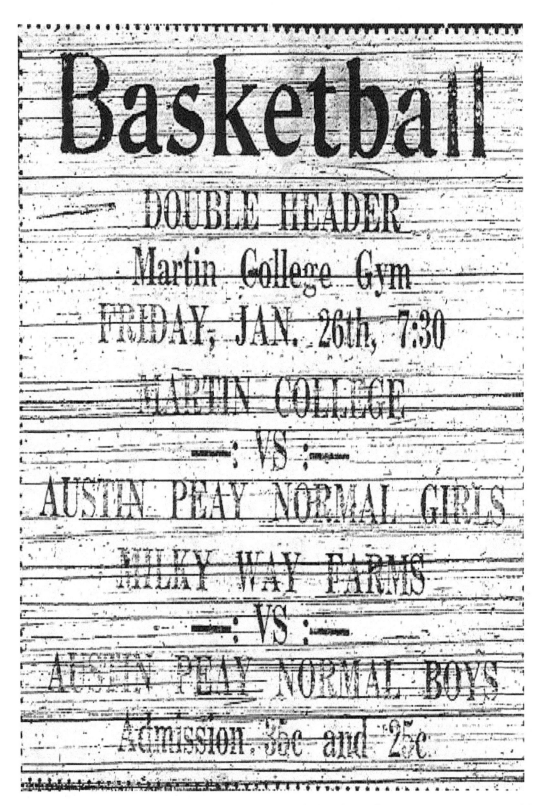

These ads in the local newspaper show examples of who the Milky Way Farms team would play.

FINANCIAL STATEMENT MILKY WAY FARMS ATHLETIC CLUB

```
Meals Collinwood Players--Paid By S.T.Collins Jr--------------$ 7.30
Entrance Fee To Tournament--Paid By Smith---------------------  2.00
Advance For Players Paid By Smith-----------------------------  10.00
  "     "     "     "     Paid By Collins-------------------  5.00
Supper for Players at Tornament --Paid by Collins-------------  2.00
                              --Paid By Phillips-------------  1.85
Total Expenses Athletic Club---------------------------------$28.15
```

-----------DONATIONS------   T
NAME   AMOUNT

NAME	AMOUNT	
	$2.50	Paid
mark Peak	2.50	Paid
Joseph Reid	2.50	Paid
	250	Paid
	250	Paid
	2.50	Paid
Peters	250	Paid
	2.50	Paid

This is an example of what it cost to operate the basketball team. Notice the donations on the bottom half of the ledger sheet.

DEPARTMENT OF COMMERCE

BUREAU OF FOREIGN AND DOMESTIC COMMERCE

WASHINGTON

April 4, 1934.

Mr S T Collins
MILKY WAY
Pulaski

My dear Mr Collins:-

It was mighty good of you to take time to write
me on a beautiful Easter Sunday when you should have been hunting
eggs and rabbits with your gal, but am sure you made up for lost time
when you did get there.

I don't suppose there was anyone more interested in
the success of the sale than I and was certainly gratified to bread
in the columns of the good old Maury Democrat that it was the outstanding
event in the South since Andrew Jackson's duel.   There was never any
doubt in my mind but that you would have the crowd and I hope you had
enough pig to go around and if so, you must have been a magician.

The work here is exceedingly interesting, but it is
mighty hard for me to wean myself from home and from Milky Way and I
am not promising to do it.   If I do nothing more than stay here for
a few months, I think it will have been worth-while.

I hope the removal of Mr Mars' to Baltimore does not
mean that his condition is worse.   If there is anything I can do
let me know, since I am within about an hour's ride of Johns Hopkins,

As I told Mr Smith in a former letter, the office
force was most appreciative of the generous shipment of candy and are
enthusiastic Milky Way boosters now.   Thank him again for me.

It does my heart and soul good to know that the catalogue
was such a success, since we did our very best on it.   With Tommy on the
job, don't forget that the office can give as good or better service than
when I was there and you know, that's going some.   Your letter was very
much appreciated and I hope you will have the time and impulse to do it
again.   Give my best to your associates, be careful about that one-arm
driving and I hope to be seeing you soon.

Sincerely,

A.B. Sowell

This letter from A.B. Sowell inquires about Mr. Mars' health, remember he used to be at the Maury Democrat in Columbia.

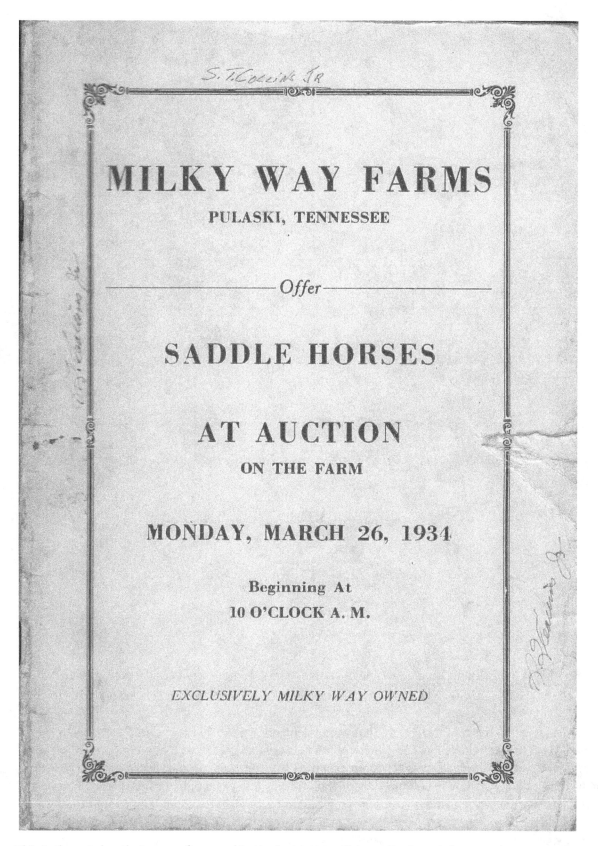

MILKY WAY FARMS

PULASKI, TENNESSEE

———— *Offer* ————

SADDLE HORSES

AT AUCTION

ON THE FARM

MONDAY, MARCH 26, 1934

Beginning At
10 O'CLOCK A. M.

EXCLUSIVELY MILKY WAY OWNED

This is the catalog that was referenced in the last letter. This particular catalog was the personal copy of S.T. Collins Jr. This catalog contains the price paid and who the buyer was.

This was a big deal to handle this line of clothing in the commissary at Milky Way.

So far we have followed a lot of things that were taking place at Milky Way Farms. It has been interesting to talk about the fast paced growth of the farm and all the things that were happening rapid fire. The other major happening was Mr. Mars' health. His health was in major decline. On April 8, 1934 he died of kidney failure in Baltimore Maryland. He was fifty years old. His final resting place was Lakewood Cemetery in Minneapolis Minnesota but before he was laid to rest in Minneapolis there was another series of events that took place. Toward the evening of his life, Mr. Mars selected a beautiful spot westward from the clubhouse and asked his family to see that he was laid to rest there when his time came. He had the location registered as a cemetery so that in the future even if the farm changed hands the cemetery would remain intact. His request to be laid to rest on that spot was granted.

Mr. and Mrs. Mars standing on the front steps of the first clubhouse.

Since we are looking at Mr. and Mrs. Mars on the steps of the first clubhouse this will be a good place to show this Milky Way Farms horse van in front of the first clubhouse.

In July of 1934 Mrs. Mars decided to honor her husband by building a mausoleum on the grounds he had chosen for his burial spot. The architectural motif was mediaeval English dating back to the year 1200. The outstanding and unusual feature of the construction of the mausoleum was the combining of the light buff limestone quarried from a developed open ledge on the farm and a pale salmon toned New England granite. The interior was a solid granite floor above which was the catacombs, six in all of Tennessee marble. A marble altar stood at the rear of the vestibule. The doors and all other metal parts were made of United States Standard Bronze. A gothic style window was built into the rear and a colored art glass depicting an inspirational scene and was set into the frame of the window and was protected by bullet proof glass and a bronze grille on the outer side. The mausoleum was completed in early November 1934.

Mausoleum.

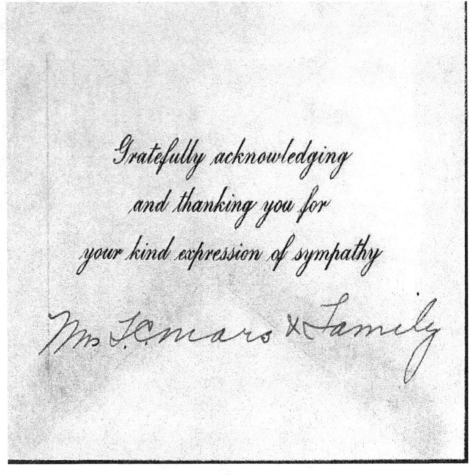

Gratefully acknowledging
and thanking you for
your kind expression of sympathy

Mr. T. C. Mars & Family

Sam T. Collins Jr. received this card of thanks for the flowers he sent to Mr. Mars' funeral.

MARS *Incorporated*

2019 to 2059 North Oak Park Ave.
Chicago, Illinois

May 21, 1934.

Mr. G.A.Smith,
MILKY WAY Farm,
Pulaski, Tennessee.

Dear Mr. Smith:

We are enclosing a photograph of Mr. Mars.

Some of our employees who wanted this picture of Mr. Mars
received one of them.

Kindly advise how many you would like us to send to you
for the employees of the MILKY WAY Farm.

Yours very truly,

MARS INCORPORATED.

BY:
Sales Department.

ASH:DJB.
Encl.

The employees at Milky Way Farms and members of the local community mourned the death of Frank
Mars and wanted a picture to remember him by.

After Mr. Mars death Mrs. Mars began to be more visible to the public. In the beginning of our story about Milky Way Farms Mrs. Mars was in the background and Mr. Mars was in the forefront. Well, all of that changed with the death of Frank C. Mars. I made a rather large point of the fact that Mr. Mars liked gaited horses and road horses. However, Mrs. Mars had bought 100 thoroughbred yearlings to be moved to the farm in anticipation of having a string of race horses. After Mr. Mars death she was off and running (just a play on words). It wasn't very long until the gaited and road horse stables would be replaced with race horses. By this time Garland Smith was the farm manager (he was married to my mother's younger sister). Mrs. Mars instructed him to announce a sale in early April of 1935 of fine blooded horses at Milky Way Farms. A smaller sale had been held in 1934 that was well attended by representatives of each part of the country. This sale was touted as the best in the country and would outstretch the earlier sale.

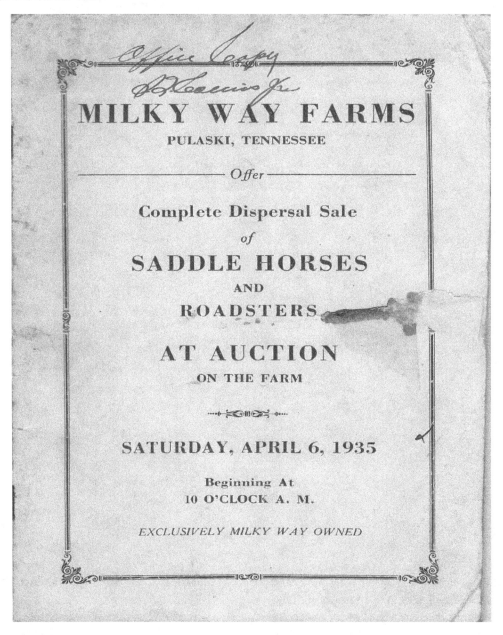

This was the dispersal sale that was just mentioned. Each buyer and sale price was written inside.

This sale would make room at the farm for the thoroughbreds that Mrs. Mars had up to this time been stabled in Santa Anita, California. These race horses along with the other yearlings would all but replace the other fine horse stock that was originally at the farm. All of the saddle horses would not be sold because Mrs. Mars liked to entertain and have ladies out to tour the farm on horseback.

Mrs. Mars enjoyed betting on the horses. Sam Collins handled the book at the farm and placed the bets with Paul Goldberg in Nashville.

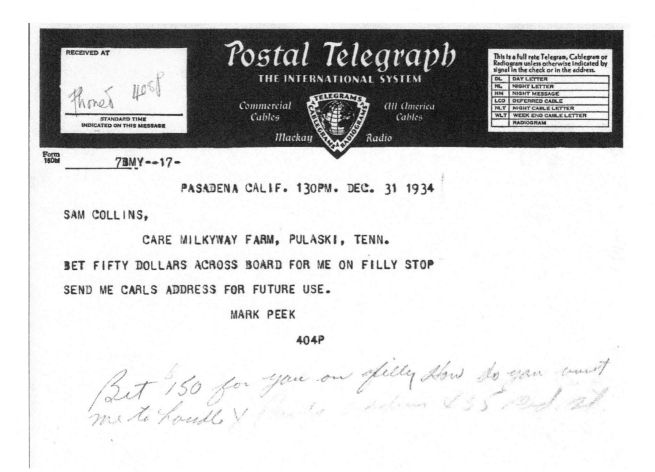

Sam Collins handled the bets for many farm employees, evidence this telegram from Mark Peek.

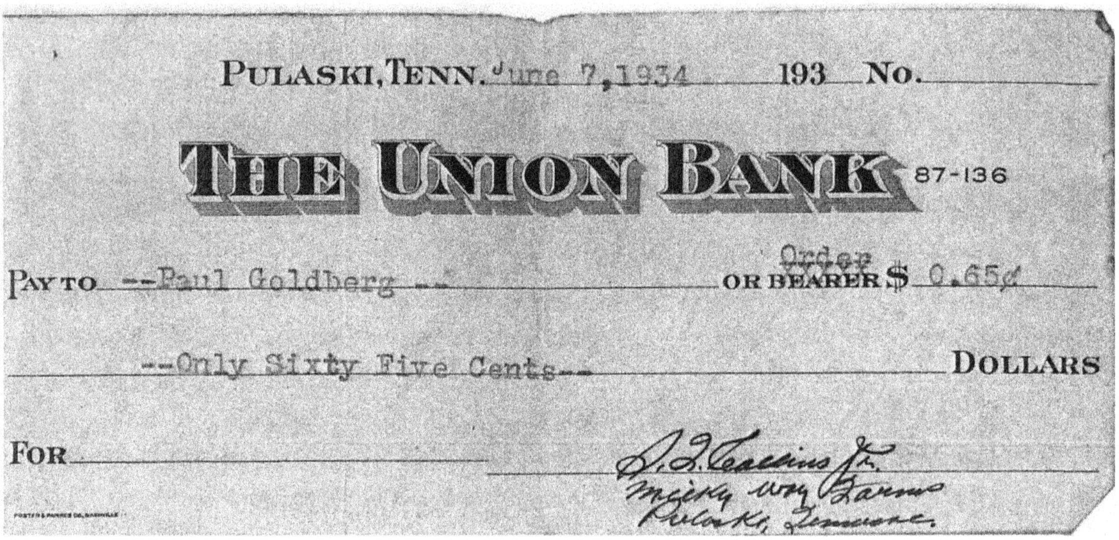

PULASKI, TENN. June 7, 1934 193 NO.

THE UNION BANK 87-136

PAY TO --Paul Goldberg-- Order OR ~~BEARER~~ $ 0.65¢

--Only Sixty Five Cents-- DOLLARS

FOR

Milky Way Farms
Pulaski, Tennessee.

Sometimes the exchanges with Mr. Goldberg weren't large enough to break the bank.

Jan.21,1938.

Mrs.Ethel V.Mars
4712 North Bay Road
Miami Beach,Fla.

Dear Mrs.Mars:

I am enclosing herewith statement of your account thru
January 14th.,and draft in the amount of $409.60.As you
will note from the statement this does not include your
winnings of January 13th.,on Murph and Daybreak which
amounted to $177.50.

I am also enclosing statement of Mrs.Feeney's account
and draft in the amount of $131.85 this covers all the
winnings due her to date.

How are you all getting along?I hope everyone is just fine
and I know you are enjoying grand weather.It has been very
nice here until today,and it has been raining very hard
all morning.Everything is just fine here.

Give my best regards to everyone.

Kindest personal regards,

                                        Sammy

The account that is being referred to is Mrs. Mar's account with the bookie in Nashville, Paul Goldberg.

Feb.19,1938.

Mrs.Ethel V.Mars
4712 North Bay Road
Miami Beach,Fla.

Dear Mrs.Mars:

How are you feeling? I hope you are just fine.Everything
is just fine here.It rained all day yesterday,but it is
chilly here today and the weatherman says that it will be
much colder tomorrow.How is Mrs.Feeny and the baby?

I am enclosing a copy of your statement thru yesterday.It
looks like we can't win a bet on Banner Man.I thought he
was a cinch yesterday.Maybe we will get even on him the
next time he starts.I surely hope the track will be dry
Tuesday so Tiger can run in the Derby.I think he will win
it.I am really going to be pulling for him.Mrs.Mars,Goldberg
says he would like to have some money so that is the
reason I mailed you your statement.

Here's hoping that Tigers carries the Milky Way Silks to
Victory in the Derby.

Kindest personal regards,

Tiger was Milky Way Farms hope for the derby in 1938. This also asks about Patty's baby.

Patty and her baby.

HOME OF
REGISTERED HEREFORD CATTLE
THOROUGHBRED HORSES

PULASKI, TENNESSEE

No. 4712 North Bay Road,
Miami Beach, Florida,
February 21st, 1938.

Mr. Sam Collins,
Milky Way Farms,
Pulaski, Tennessee.

Dear Mr. Collins:

Mrs. Mars has asked me to send to you the enclosed check payable to the order of cash in the amount of $840.00 covering her account with Goldberg, as per your letter of the 19th instant.

Yes, to-day is the day and we are hoping that TIGER will come through with flying colors.

With kind regards, I am

Sincerely,

Ethel H. Storck

Ethel Storck wrote a lot of correspondence for Mrs. Mars. She was her constant companion.

HOME OF
REGISTERED HEREFORD CATTLE
THOROUGHBRED HORSES

PULASKI, TENNESSEE

Louisville, Ky.
167 Pindell
April 23,.1938

Mr. S.T.Collins Jr.
Milkyway Farms
Pulaski, Tenn.

Dear Sam?

        Well here I lay in bed no pains no tempaature just
got to layvhere until this old bone growsb back together
        Mrs Mars sure has been nice to me she has written to
me every day and has said things to me that have kept me from
worring about my job. I've got a lot to tell you Sam when I
see you. I hope you can come to thr derby, you can stay at my house
we have plenty of room if some of you do have to sleep on the
floor, we would be more than glad to have you.

        I guess Tigerv isnout ofb the derby as he has a bad
foot. Mr. Morriss comes by about every day and gives me the dope
on the horses. He seems to think that Tiger has a broken bone
in his foot but he isn't sure but if he has he will be out for
some time.

        Mountain Ridge is running at Keeneland today and he is
the only hopes that we have in the Ky. Derby but it is an open
race I will name you the first five in the derby as to my
opinion and see how far I am off: Mountain Ridge, Fighting Fox
Stagehand, Dauber Bull Leaand Gov/ Chandler

        What I mean about these five is that theybwill finish
in the money not saying what position.
        Write me when you have time , excuse all these miss
keys as I am lieing in bed.

                Best regards to all

                        Your friend

                        Neely

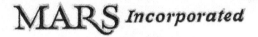

MARS *Incorporated*

XXXXX XX XXXXXNXXXXXXXXXXXXXXXX
XXXXXXXXXXXXXXXX

Pulaski,Tennessee.

May 6,1935

Mr.Paul Goldberg
435 Deaderick St.
Nashville,Tennessee.

Dear Paul:

I am enclosing herewith the following receipts that we
hold on the future books of the Ky.Derby which you placed
for us will you kindly collect same for me and send the
money to me:

```
Dr.J.E.Peters Entry $2.00 To Show------------------$16.00
XXXXXXXXX
Mark Peak--Whiskolo $5.00 To Show------------------ 50.00
S.T.Collins Jr.--Entry 50.00 To Show--------------400.00
Mrs.Ethel V.Mars-Entry 100.00 To Show-------------300.00
Mrs.Ethel V.Mars-Whiskolo 10.00 To Show----------- 80.00
Mrs.E.L.Savage-Whiskolo 2.00 To Show-------------- 16.00
Mrs.E.L.Savage-Entry 2.00 to Show----------------- 6.00
Total------------------------------------------$868.00

Dr.J.E.Peters Receipt from Paul Goldberg Entry
$2.00 to Show----------------------------------- 6.00
                                              $874.00
```

I will certainly appreciate it if you will collect these for
me and return the money tome.

Very Truly Yours,

S.T.Collins Jr.

"When you crave good candy—Milky Way"

Sometimes the bets were larger. Notice who bet the most.

Pulaski, Tenn.
December 20, 1934

Mr. John Yocum, Mgr.
Express Traffic Pa. RR.
Philadelphia, Pa.

Dear Sir:-

        I want to thank you for the nice picture
you sent me of the horse car No. 5834 named Milky
Way Farms. As you know we used this car recently in
shipping some of our Race Horses to the west coast.
This was a very nice car and was satisfactory in
every respect except that it needed some padding in
it. We appreciate very much the fact that this
car was named Milky Way Farms and we will be glad
to use it in making future shipments when it is at
all possible to do so. Again thanking you for the
picture.

                    Yours very truly

                        MILKY WAY FARMS

                        BY
                            G. A. SMITH

GAS/c

When you were Milky Way Farms a railroad would put your name on a special car.

Pulaski, Tenn.
December 27, 1934

Manager Brown Hotel
Louisville, Ky.

Dear Sir:-

        Will you kindly reserve a suite of
rooms for Mrs. Ethel V. Mars during the week of
the Kentucky Derby?   Kindly advise us concerning the above?

                        Yours very truly

                        MILKY WAY FARMS

                            BY
                                S. T. COLLINS, JR.

STC/c

Sam Collins handled Mrs. Mars reservations for the Derby.

THE *Brown* HOTEL

LOUISVILLE, KENTUCKY

From the office of
HAROLD E. HARTER
Manager

December 29, 1934

Mr. S. T. Collins, Jr.
Milky Way Farms
Pulaski, Tennessee

Dear Mr. Collins:

We acknowledge with thanks your letter of December 27 and are delighted to learn that Mrs. Ethel V. Mars anticipates attending the Kentucky Derby, 1935.

In accordance with your request it is our pleasure to enter Mrs. Mars' reservation for a suite during this period, and after the first of the year when the arrangements for this event are completed we will write you relative to the rates, dates, etc.

Again thanking you and assuring you of our most interested efforts toward Mrs. Mars' comfort while with us, we are

Very truly yours,

THE BROWN HOTEL

M. H. Jones
Assistant Manager

mhj;af

The Brown Hotel was happy to accommodate Mrs. Mar's request.

Beverly Hills, Calif.
805 N. Crescent Drive.
February 12, 1935.

Mr. Sam T. Collins Jr.
Milky Way Farm.
Pulaski, Tenn.

My dear Sammy,

I am glad you took care of the reservations at the Brown Hotel in Louisville for the Derby.

I shall probably require more room than they have reserved and I have taken the matter up with Mark Peak who has of course had some correspondence with them.

I wish to be on one of the top floors to avoid the noise and the letter to you does not signify on which floor they have made reservations. I think Mark is taking care of this but I wish to thank you for your interest.

With kindest wishes, I am,

Sincerely,

Ethel V. Mars

Ethel V. Mars.

EVM/hcr

Apparently Mrs. Mars thought that Mark Peak had more experience with reservations.

Mrs. Mars was an avid rider in her own right.

Mrs. Mars and friends on a social ride on the farm.

Another ride on what would be today, Milky Way Farms Road. The small houses in the background were used for employees. After the sale of the farm most of those houses were moved to Pulaski.

April 6, 1935 was the day that the fine blooded saddle horses were put on the block. It was estimated that 4,000 people came to the sale. There were representatives from all over the country in attendance. Before the sale started lunch was served by the Giles County Parent Teachers Association. The sale started at one o'clock. The champion gelding, Calumet Armistlee, topped the sale at $7,000. A Milky Way Farms employee, Mark Peak, bought his favorite horse, Signal Flash, at $4,000. When the sale was over at about five o'clock, forty-eight of the choicest horses in the south had been purchased for $36,000. As I have already mentioned this was a dispersal sale of fancy show horses that had been bred and trained at Milky Way Farms. Mrs. Mars kept a few choice animals for she and her friends to ride. The move to thoroughbred horses at Milky Way Farms was complete. Even though Mr. Mars had bought a few race horse colts before his death and Mrs. Mars had added to that number, he would have never considered the wholesale sell off of his prized saddle horses.

Calumet Armistlee was one of Mr. Mars favorite show horses.

August 15, 1935, Mrs. Mars went to the highly touted horse sale at Saratoga Springs, N.Y. and bought a group of five fillies and colts for $20,700. She also made the record purchase of the entire sale when she paid $13,000 for a brown-gray colt by Victorian Grief.

These young men were grooms, it was their job to leg these colts up.

On Monday March 9, 1936 Milky Way Farms sold the top selling load of cattle on the Chicago market. It was widely believed that this was the first time a load of Tennessee cattle had ever commanded the days top price. The load consisted of Hereford steers that had been fed at the farm in Pulaski. The load averaged 1373 pounds and sold for $11.65 per cwt or $159.95 per head. These cattle were accompanied to market by Garland A. Smith who was at that time in charge of cattle feeding at Milky Way Farms. Some 2,000 to 3,000 high grade steers were annually fattened for market at the farm. These cattle were fed on ground shelled corn and molasses. Many of these steers were purchased out west and shipped to the farm. All of these cattle were not raised at Milky Way Farms. Remember that the farm was known for its herd of Hereford cattle and purebred Shorthorns.

This is one of the Domino strain of horned Herefords that Alan Feeney bought as a buyer for Milky Way Farms and had shipped to the farm.

Steers on feed at Milky Way Farms feed lots.

One of the purebred Hereford barns.

What a beautiful view of a Hereford barn.

The feed lots and barns were full getting ready to ship cattle to Chicago.

Milky Way Farms cattle on feed were closely monitored for quality.

Milky Way Farms quality on the rail.

HERD SIRES—MILKY WAY FARMS, PULASKI, TENN.

1—Colorado Domino 159th 2317433   2—Prince Domino Aster 2888888   3—Colorado Domino E 303 2964362   4—M.W. Domino 25th 2868154   5—Domino Deluxe 2972834
6—M.W. Domino 32nd 2972832   7—Milky Way Mixer Domino 2861614   8—Milky Way Tommy Domino 14th 2569773   9—M.W. Anxiety 34th 2972821   10—Larry Domino 50th 2624412

Milky Way Farms Herd Sires

CHAMPION HEIFERS EXHIBITED BY MILKY WAY FARMS, DURING THE PAST FIVE YEARS
Milky Way Farms   Pulaski, Tennessee

1—Milky Way Donna Domino 2488818   2—MW Blue Bell 6th 3049626   3—MW Miss Domino 54th 3290229   4—MW Domineta 23d 2797207
5—Lady Larryana 2902008   6—MW Princess Domino 48th 286185   7—Milky Way Domineta 10th 2569779   8—MW Domineta 20th 2749735

Champion Heifers

Milky Way Farms had a grade "A" dairy that featured the largest herd of Holstein cows in the mid-state.

This dairy barn was state of the art for that time.

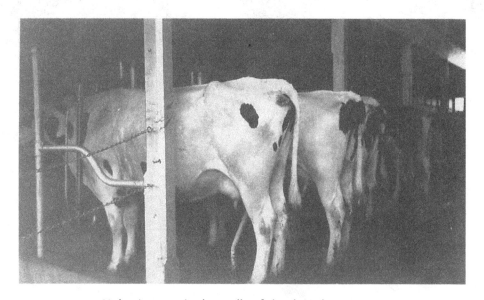

Holstein cows in the stalls of the dairy barn.

Sheep were a large part of the Milky Way Farms operation.

Notice the dog used to work sheep in the left part of the picture.

Sheep were a lot of trouble. They had to be dipped to keep the parasites off them.

Baltimore and Ohio Special Dinner $1.25
Broiled Small Sirloin Steak Dinner $1.50

[Including Appetizer, Relish, Soup, Two Vegetables,
Salad, Dessert, Beverage.]

Appetizer

Fruit Cocktail   Chilled Tomato Juice

Relish

Celery Hearts   Assorted Olives

Soup

Lobster Mulligatawney   Consomme, Clear

Entrees
Brochette of Oysters and Bacon
Braised Young Chicken with Smithfield Ham
Larded Beef Tenderloin, Natural
(Prize Beef from Baltimore Live Stock Show)

Vegetables
Whipped Potatoes   Candied Sweet Potatoes
Brussels Sprouts   Green Peas, Butter Sauce   String Beans

Salad
Lettuce and Tomato Salad
Baltimore and Ohio Dressing

Dessert
Green Apple Pie with Cheese
Ice Cream   Sliced Orange
Choice of Cheese, Plain or Toasted Crackers

Beverage
Coffee   Tea   Kaffee Hag   Instant Postum   Cocoa
Individual Milk or Buttermilk

Fish or Eggs Substituted for Meat if Desired

DEER PARK (MARYLAND) SPRING WATER IS USED EXCLUSIVELY

Passengers are respectfully requested to write orders on checks,
as waiters are forbidden to take verbal orders

Passengers will please consult Steward if the service is not entirely to their satisfaction

For sale of Beer, passengers will please consult Beverage Card

Passengers Are Requested Not To Smoke In Dining Car

F. A. STINE
Manager of Dining Car and
Commissary Department
Baltimore, Maryland

Steward of Car

LA-4

Milky Way Farms provided fed cattle that ended up on menus like this one of the Baltimore and Ohio
Railroad.

AUCTION SALE

— AT —

Milky Way Farms

Pulaski, Tenn.

Tuesday, June 22, 1937

Sale Starts At 1:00 P. M.

40 Head of the Choicest
Scotch Shorthorn Cattle

that will be sold anywhere this year.

16 Outstanding Herd Bulls   24 Choice Females

The finest opportunity that has ever been offered for farmers of the South to obtain richly bred Shorthorn cattle. These are the kind of cattle that really fit into a successful agricultural program. Prices are increasing. Buy now and make big profits.

Write for this sale catalog and plan to attend

MILKY WAY FARMS

Pulaski, Tenn.

Most locals will tell you that they do not remember the shorthorn cattle but they were there and contributed greatly to the national prominence of the farm.

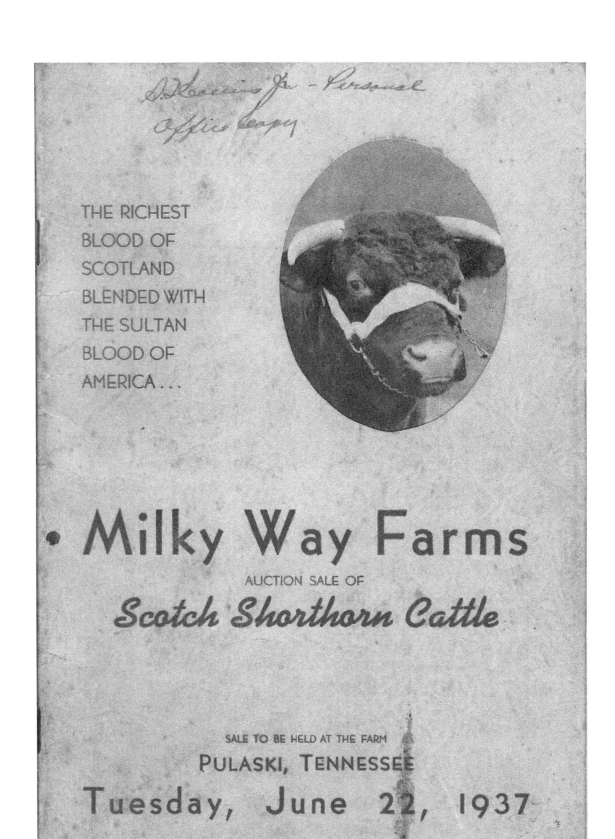

THE RICHEST
BLOOD OF
SCOTLAND
BLENDED WITH
THE SULTAN
BLOOD OF
AMERICA...

• Milky Way Farms

AUCTION SALE OF

Scotch Shorthorn Cattle

SALE TO BE HELD AT THE FARM

PULASKI, TENNESSEE

Tuesday, June 22, 1937

The catalog for the June 22, 1937 sale of Shorthorn cattle at Milky Way Farms.

SEVERAL YEARS AGO, when Milky Way Farms selected five wonderful stock bulls from the most noted herds in Scotland and brought them to this country to head their great herd, breeders everywhere began looking forward to the time when the produce of these matings would be available. Students of the breed were well aware of the fact that the Milky Way herd had been founded largely on the intensely bred Avondale and Whitehall Sultan females which were acquired through the purchase of the entire famous herds of Anoka Farms and Hearts Delight Farms. Now comes the announcement that this combination of the best blood of two continents is available and 37 head, all but one bred by Milky Way Farms, will be offered at public auction at this world renowned farm on June 22d. Here indeed is an outstanding lot of cattle, with many show prospects and every one rich in quality, type and character. A study of the pedigrees that are listed in this catalog will be convincing proof of the desirability of these cattle as foundation units, and every animal has inherited the character and style that can result only from strong ancestry. This is one of the top offerings of the year and breeders may make long trips to this sale with full assurance that they will find the kind of cattle that are worthy of such an investment.—Hal Longley of The Shorthorn World.

This page was inside the catalog. It helps shed some light on the shorthorn operation at Milky Way Farms. I know that I am making a big deal of the shorthorns but they need to be recognized for their importance and so many people want to deny their existence at the farm. Notice the mention of Hearts Delight Farm.

That same month twelve carloads of prime cattle from the farm were shipped by rail to Hoboken, N.J. for the eastern markets. Four cars of lambs were also shipped to the same point. It was believed that representatives of the Cudahy Packing Company bought both shipments. On Tuesday, June 22, 1937 Milky Way Farms held a sale of forty head of the choicest scotch shorthorn cattle that was to be sold anywhere that year. Sixteen outstanding herd bulls and 24 choice females were offered at 1:00 p.m. at the farm. The Pulaski Citizen on October 16, 1940 ran an article about Milky Way Farms at the International: "Tennessee's first entries for the 1940 International Livestock Exposition and Horse Show were made this week by Milky Way Farms at Pulaski, Giles County. They have listed entries for a show herd of fifteen purebred shorthorn cattle. Milky Way Farms, owned by Mrs. Ethel Mars, of Chicago have been prominently represented at the Chicago show in recent years by many of the top prize winners in the shorthorn cattle competitions." Further proof of the shorthorn cattle operation at the farm. The horned Hereford operation was pushed by Allen Feeney, the husband of Patty.

The farm had its own railroad spur across the "Bee Line Highway" not far from the overpass.

As the farm grew in prominence in the cattle feeding world so was their fame in the race horse circles. In March of 1936 Whiskolo, a four year old son of Diavolo, made his first start of the year and carried the silks of Milky Way Farms to their second straight victory in the feature race at Arlington Downs when he captured the Denison purse. The Fighter won the inaugural handicap for Mrs. Mars in a previous race.

The Fighter.

Wonderful Nite.

Sangreal.

"FOREVER YOURS"
GR. FZ TORO - WINSOME WAY
MILKY WAY FARM

Forever Yours was Mrs. Mars favorite thoroughbred.

Mrs. Mars had this inset with forever yours.

"FOREVER YOURS" W.D. WRIGHT UP
WINNER "THE SPINAWAY" SARATOGA AUG. 17, 1935
"PARADE GIRL" 2ND "TONY'S WIFE" 3RD

Forever Yours after winning the "Spinaway"

Churchill Downs 5-4-40   "Gallahadion"   W. Bierman-Up
Owner Milky Way Farms

You have seen many pictures of Gallahadion. This is the original picture after the Derby. The ones you see with Mrs. Mars in the inset were added at a later date. She was not at the Derby that day.

In October 1937 Sam Collins got an offer that he felt like he couldn't refuse. A new bank was being formed in Pulaski and he was offered the opportunity to be the assistant cashier at a starting salary of $100.00 a month. He would also have to sell some stock and buy some himself. Dr. W. J. Johnson was to be the president and Riggs Harwell was to be the cashier. This bank would later become the First National Bank in Pulaski, Tennessee. This would be a big decision because he loved Milky Way Farms. He tendered his resignation to Mrs. Mars and prepared to sell his allotted bank stock and get ready for his new job. His wife, Christine, did not want to leave the farm. After much discussion with his wife of two years and Mrs. Mars he decided not to leave the place that he loved for the insecurity of the opening of a new bank in the midst of the depression. After all where else could he earn $175.00 a month, have a house furnished and a car.

ROBERT E. LEE
ATTORNEY
PULASKI, TENN.

October 2, 1937

Mr. S. T. Collins
Milky Way Farms
Pulaski, Tennessee

Dear Sam:

Dr. W. J. Johnson has agreed to take $10,000.00 worth of stock in the new bank stock and act as president; Riggs Harwell of the Cornersville bank, has agreed to take $5,000.00 worth of stock and act as cashier.

I have put your name before the promoters and they have agreed with me to elect you assistant cashier, at a salary to begin with around a $100.00. They would expect you to take some stock, and I told them you would take ten shares and get out and sell some. I have already had a conversation with the Superintendent of Banks and it appears that he will act favorably on our application for a charter. A bunch of us are going back to see him next Thursday or Friday. I am enclosing herewith a subscription list for you to sign and get as many names thereon as you can by next Wednesday night, and bring the same down home.

Be sure to report to me by next Wednesday night your progress.

Yours truly,

REL:as

This letter nearly caused Sam Collins to leave the job he loved.

December 9,1937.

Mrs.Ethel V.Mars
930 Ashland Ave.
River Forest,Ill.

My Dear Mrs.Mars:

How are you feeling ? I hope you are just fine.The
weather has been rather cold here this week.We had
about two inches of snow yesterday.

Mrs.Mars herewith tender you my resignation to become
effective December 31st..I have accepted a position
as Assistant Cashier in a new bank that is being
organized in Pulaski.Mrs.Mars you do not know how very
much I do appreciate the many nice things you have
done for me.You have been simply wonderful to me in
every way.And again I want to tell you how very much
I do appreciate it.

I am looking forward to seeing you in a few days.I want
to talk to you when you arrive here and have time to
see me.

With kindest regards,

                                        Sammy

A resignation letter that he thought he would never write.

HOME OF
REGISTERED HEREFORD CATTLE
THOROUGHBRED HORSES

PULASKI, TENNESSEE

Dec.24th.1937.

I have decided to keep Samuel Collins Jr. in my employ for the next
six years at least and probably longer, providing his services are
satisfactory. He is privaliged to leave if he wishes with a reasonable
advance notice. I shall give him a bonus each year, contingent on
theFarm's sucess.

Ethel V. Mars

Mrs. Mars extended Sam Collins employment for six years and he decided not to leave the farm for the
new bank being established in Pulaski.

MARS *Incorporated*

2019 to 2059 North Oak Park Ave.
Chicago, Illinois

January 6, 1938

Mr. S. T. Collins, Jr.,
Milky Way Farms,
Pulaski, Tenn.

Dear Mr. Collins:

As per instructions from Mrs. Mars, your salary

will be $175.00 per month, effective January 1, 1938.

Yours truly,

MARS INCORPORATED

By: *G. B. Hurley*
          G. B. Hurley

GBH*VG

Mrs. Mars raised his pay to a figure he could not refuse.

When it came to the clubhouse staff Mrs. Mars wanted to personally make sure that the people that were hired were the type that would reflect positively on the farm.

HOME OF
REGISTERED HEREFORD CATTLE
THOROUGHBRED HORSES

PULASKI, TENNESSEE

January 15th, 1938.

Mr. Sam Smith,
Milky Way Farms,
Pulaski, Tennessee.

Dear Sammy:

Am sorry I didn't get to see you to-day to say goodbye but you can write me at my Miami Beach address.

You may start Mrs. Neill's salary from the day on which she came, which I think was Tuesday, at the same salary with which we started Mrs. Pridemore. In order not to make the bookkeeping too confusing you may pay her when you do the rest of the help and figure the salary she has coming accordingly.

Please notify the Chicago office that I wish them to send a _new_ typewriter for our use in this office.

Any housekeeper applications which come to the office please forward to me at Florida.

With kindest personal regards, I am

Very sincerely,

EVM/S

EVM/S is Ethel V. Mars by Ethel Storck, her personal secretary. She got confused about who the letter was being sent to.

HORSES IN CALIFORNIA

1. The Fighter

2. Wise Daughter

3. Gallaclay

4. Gallerne

5. Irksome

6. Double Four

7. Handmade

8. Reelon

9. Torolee

10. Caliban

11. The Persian

12. Jaw Breaker

13. Murph

14. DOGAWAY -------------------- Bull Dog--Runaway Lass

15. FAST EXPRESS -------------- Clock Tower Possible

16. Reaping Reward

17. HOWDY ANDY ----------------Sir Andrew--Imp.La Deliverance

18. ANCESTRAL ----------------- Crucifixion--Ascunatrad

19. SKEETSHOOTER ------------- Diavolo--Pop Gun

20. Not Asleep

21. Mindalo

22. Talma Dee

23. Miss Gravity

Milky Way Farms always had a string of horses on the road.

HOME OF
REGISTERED HEREFORD CATTLE
THOROUGHBRED HORSES

PULASKI, TENNESSEE

(At) 120 Union Avenue,
Saratoga Springs, New York,
August 9th, 1938.

Mr. Sam Collins,
Milky Way Farms,
Pulaski, Tennessee.

My dear Sam:

Lord knows I should have written to you sooner than this to thank you for your lovely letter that you wrote me while in Chicago when I first returned from the farm but really one could not appreciate what Mrs. Mars has gone through since returning from the farm and it seems just when I think I will have a few minutes to myself something else turns up and I find that I have been extremely lax in my personal correspondence. However, I have tried to tell you personally, Sam, how much I have appreciated your cooperation and the many kindnesses you have extended to me.

Again, I am afraid, I will have to ask a favor - I am trying to get up for Mrs. Mars a comprehensive race horse book so that we do not have to carry around so much correspondence. I talked to Neely at the house this afternoon, thinking he might have the information I want, but he advised me he does not have it and suggested my writing to you. This is what I would like to have if not too much trouble simply the total, without any detail, of the cost of running the stable and winnings in 1935, 1936. I have the record for 1937 which Neely has given me which according to his figures were as follows:

Expenses	$ 242,250.39
Winnings	214,640.00

If these figures are not correct I would appreciate your advising me the correct figures.

We have not been to the track nor the sales since our arrival as Mrs. Mars was not feeling very well yesterday although I am happy to say she is feeling a little better to-day.

With kindest regards to you always and thanking you again, I am

Sincerely,

Ethel H. Storck

Miss Storck was trying to find out if the horses were profitable or not.

August 16,1936.

Miss Ethel H.Storck
120 Union Avenue
Saratoga Springs,New York.

My Dear Miss Storck:

Was glad to receive your letter.I know you must have been
thru lots in the last few weeks.I surely hope Mrs.Mars is
feeling lots better.She has been thru so much.I surely
have felt so sorry for her.

I was so glad that Dinner Date won the Spinaway.I surely
hope that we can win some more of the Two Year old Stakes
down there this fall.Looks like we might have a fair chance
in some of them too.

I have check my records for 1935 and 1936 and the following
is the amount of Winnings and Expenses:

            1935---Winnings $108,090.00
                   Expenses $139,147.18

            1936---Winnings $211,953.75
                   Expenses $168,366.98

Anytime that I can be of any help to you do not fail to call
on me for I am only too glad to do anything I can.Everything
is going good here.We are getting ready for the big Dairy
Festival to be held this week-end.It is really going to be
something nice.Wish you were here to see it.

Give my kindest regards to Mrs.Mars,and best personal regards
to you,I am

                                        Sincerely,

1936 was a good year, 1935 not so much.

(At) 120 Union Avenue,
Saratoga Springs, New York,
August 18th, 1938.

Mr. Sam Collins,
Milky Way Farms,
Pulaski, Tennessee.

My dear Sam:

Thank you for your letter of the 16th instant received this afternoon giving me the winnings and expenses of the racing stable for the years 1935 and 1936. In discussing this with Mrs. Mars this afternoon she told me that she actually started the racing stable in 1934 and if it is not too much trouble I would appreciate your giving me the winnings and expenses for 1934.

Mrs. Mars is, I believe, feeling a little better but I am afraid that nothing but perfect rest and relaxation can help her. We have been to the races twice and the sales three evenings and outside of that we haven't done a thing but work at the house. It has been terribly hot here for the past three days and it was almost impossible to do anything.

DINNER DATE ran a grand race and this is one of the days that we were there and it surely gave us a big thrill as we know it did you from the lovely wire you sent to Mrs. Mars.

I extended your kindest regards to Mrs. Mars and as I am writing to you she is sitting opposite me and she asked me to remember her to you.

With kindest regards, I am

Sincerely,

This letter confirms that the racing stable was started in 1934 after Mr. Mars death. Remember that after Mr. Mars death the focus went from gaited and road horses to race horses. Also, the emphasis moved from shorthorn cattle to horned Herefords.

Aug.25,1938.

Miss Ethel H.Storck
120 Union Avenue
Saratoga Springs,N.Y.

My Dear Miss Storck:

I am only too glad to give you the winnings and expenses
for the racing stable for 1934 they are as follows:

         Winnings $17,210.00

         Expenses $52,053.63

The horses surely are doing fine down there.I surely was
thrilled when No Competition and Giles County won the
stakes.You know I think GILES COUNTY will win the Derby
next year.He has such a good name he just has to win it.Ha:Ha.

I hope Mrs.Mars is much improved.You tell her to be sure
and take lots of rest.I am really going to be pulling for
us to win the HOPEFUL,and I hope we can repeat in it this
year.

Give my kindest regards to Mrs.Mars,and best personal regards
to you,I am

                                        Sincerely,

1934 was not a good year for the horses.

MARS *Incorporated*

2019 to 2059 North Oak Park Ave.
Chicago, Illinois

November 1, 1938

Mr. S. T. Collins, Jr.,
Milky Way Farms,
Pulaski, Tenn.

Dear Mr. Collins:

We wish to acknowledge receipt of your letter of October 31st and are very sorry to hear of Mr. Smith's father being so seriously ill. We sincerely hope he will fully recover.

Do not know when we will get down to the Farms. It seems that you people are doing such a good job of keeping records that there is no necessity for us to come down any more. However, the writer certainly would like to make a trip to the Farms and will whenever possible.

Yours truly,

MARS INCORPORATED

By: *G. B. Hurley*

G. B. Hurley

GBH*VG

The executives at Mars Inc. looked for excuses to come to the farm. It was a refreshing change from Chicago.

HOME OF
REGISTERED HEREFORD CATTLE
THOROUGHBRED HORSES

PULASKI, TENNESSEE

(At) Ambassador Hotel,
Los Angeles, California,
February 6th, 1939.

Mr. Sam Collins,
Milky Way Farms,
Pulaski, Tennessee.

Dear Sam:

I received your letter of February 3rd this morning with the enclosed clipping from the Nashville Banner. They certainly gave us a nice send off and write-up and I should be very happy to have you send me any worth-while articles that you may see in the Nashville Banner or neighboring papers.

Miss Storck is feeling much better but has really been very ill. Her operation was more serious than we thought and her nurse left only last Thursday. The incision has healed nicely and I think within a couple of months the scar will not be noticeable.

We have only been to the races once although we have planned on going a couple of other times but it rained so hard and was so disagreeable we did not go out. We hope to go out some day this week. California has been having a little of the weather the east and south have been having, such as rain, snow and hail.

I can imagine how high the creek is if it is as high as you have ever seen it as I have seen it plenty high.

Thanking you again for the clipping and with kindest personal regards, I am

Sincere_ly,

Ethel V. Mars

EVM*S

Mrs. Mars liked to keep up with what the local and state papers were saying about her and what was going on at the farm. This is another example that she did not spend as much time at the farm as most people thought she did.

(At) Marlands,
Minocqua, Wisconsin,
July 12th, 1939.

Mr. Sam Smith,
Milky Way Farms,
Pulaski, Tennessee.

My dear Sam:

Your letter of July 10th received by me to-day was indeed a very pleasant surprise. I am feeling very much better and am thoroughly enjoying my rest up here. The weather is nice, we have had rain and, of course, we have had some hot days but nothing in comparison to what other parts of the country have had.

I was very disappointed I could not get down to the farm before coming up here but it was simply impossible. I hope the time will come that I will not have to spend a part of every year in a hospital. I am planning definitely on coming down this fall as I always enjoy that season of the year in Tennessee.

I know with all the rains that you have had that the farm must look beautiful and the pastures must be in excellent condition.

I have been pleased with the way the Herefords have been selling and with the excellent prospects that I think we have in them. I wish I could say the same for the horses. However, the year is not over and I am still hoping that we can round them into shape.

Trusting that you and Christine are both feeling fine, I am, with kindest personal regards,

Sincerely,

Ethel V. Mars

Ethel V. Mars

P. S. I gave your nice little message to Storcky and she only mentioned the other day that it had been a long time since either one of us had heard from you.

Mrs. Mars bemoaned the fact that she spent so much time in the hospital. She also wished that she could spend more time at the farm.

THE LOS ANGELES
AMBASSADOR
CALIFORNIA
April 10th, 1939.

Mr. Sam Collins,
Milky Way Farms,
Pulaski, Tennessee.

My dear Sam:

Thank you for your very nice letter of the 4th. I have refrained from answering until we returned here as I wanted to check up the financial statements received from the company and in checking same to-day I find that I can figure the winnings and expenses of the racing stable for 1938 from these statements. I had forgotten that Mrs. Mars had instructed Mr. Hurley to separate the racing stable from the farm account and this statement will now give me all the information we require for our records. It will not be necessary, therefore, Sam, for you to send me each month a copy of the invoice which you send to Mr. Hurley.

We returned from Palm Springs last Saturday evening and I am so glad to say that Mrs. Mars is feeling ever so much better for her stay on the desert. In a way, it is too bad she could not have spent a couple of weeks more there but time is growing short and we must be back in Chicago, as well as to go to Kentucky.

I can just imagine how lovely it is beginning to look at the farm and am getting rather a longing to be there and see you all.

I hope you are feeling your usual peppy self and have managed to get all of those darn bugs out of your system.

With kindest regards to you all, I am

Most sincerely,

Storcky

P. S.   Now that I have known you all for about 14 months it would be my suggestion that you and Garland call me Storcky as everyone else does. I have taken the liberty from the beginning to call you each by your first names and I feel as you consider me possibly by now as being in the one big family that it would seem more like home to be called Storcky.

VISIT THE GOLDEN GATE INTERNATIONAL EXPOSITION SAN FRANCISCO 1939

This gives the reader an idea how Mrs. Mars traveled and where they stayed. The P.S. shows that Miss Storcky wanted to be one of the guys (so to speak).

As we follow this time line of events in the history of Milky Way Farms the death of Garland Smith occurred on January 28, 1940. Garland was the farm manager and a trusted employee of Mrs. Mars. He died after a short illness with pneumonia. Garland was one of the young men engaged by Mr. Mars when he established the farm. After the death of Mr. Mars the general management of the farm was largely left to his judgment. Garland was survived by his wife, Lucille Sanders Smith, my mother's younger sister.

HOME OF
REGISTERED HEREFORD CATTLE
THOROUGHBRED HORSES

PULASKI, TENNESSEE

(At) Ambassador Hotel,
Los Angeles, California,
February 4th, 1940.

Mr. Sam Collins,
Milky Way Farms,
Pulaski, Tennessee.

My dear Sam:

      I trust that you are feeling better now and are getting hold of yourself. I am sure that the shock of losing Garland was hard on all of us. There is no question but what he will be greatly missed but as the saying is "The show must go on."

      I think you will be able to handle the office very well yourself with the aid of a stenographer. I authorized Alan by wire to have you hire one. I have also authorized Mr. Hurley to increase your salary beginning as of February 1st.

      Please let me hear from you as often as possible and let me know how everything is going.

      With the deepest sympathy to you all and wishing you the best of everything, I am

                Sincerely,

                Ethel V. Mars

EVM*S

The death of Garland Smith was a shock but Mrs. Mars trusted Sam Collins to run the farm.

2019 to 2059 North Oak Park Ave.
Chicago, Illinois

February 14, 1940

Mr. S. T. Collins, Jr.,
Milky Way Farms,
Pulaski, Tenn.

Dear Mr. Collins:

     Mrs. Mars advised that your salary was to be increased $25.00 per month. As you are now receiving $175.00 your salary will be $200.00 per month, effective February 1, 1940.

Yours truly,

MARS INCORPORATED

G. B. Hurley
Auditor

GBH*VG

Making $200.00 a month was a real achievement at this time in history.

Most people credit Gallahadion's win in the 1940 Kentucky Derby as the biggest event in Milky Way Farms history. The win was a total surprise to the book-makers and racing experts. Bimelech was expected to win and it was thought Gallahadion would finish somewhere down the line. The 66th Kentucky Derby was run on May 4, 1940. The Derby program for that day had an insert that listed the probable starters, their records and best races to April 8, 1940. Bimelech was listed as of April 8, 1940 as 2-1 and Gallahadion was listed at 50-1.

NAME OF HORSE	COLOR AND SEX	SIRE AND DAM	OWNER	1939-1940 RECORDS	WINTER BK. OD. 4/8/40	CLOSING ODDS
COCKEREL	b. c.	Transmute / Chickie	A. Untermeyer	Started 14 times as 2-year-old; won 4, second 1, third 2; won $14,775; won Pimlico Nursery Stakes, Juvenile Stakes at Belmont Park, Sagamore Stakes at Pimlico; third, Tremont Stakes at Aqueduct. Did not race during winter.	40-1	
POTRANCO	br. g.	Judge Hay / Essie Wessie	Lexbrook Stable (L. D. Kern)	Started 12 times as 2-year-old; won 6, second 2, third 1; won $12,090; Won Ravisloe Stakes at Washington Park, Labor Day Handicap at Hawthorne; second, Prairie State Stakes at Washington Park, Hawthorne Juvenile Handicap. Started 3 times as 3-year-old at Oaklawn, winning 1, unplaced 2.	40-1	
RED DOCK	b. g.	Peace Chance / Bittersweet	Greentree Stable (Mrs. Payne Whitney)	As 2-year-old, started 8; won 1, second 5, third 1; won $1,275. As 3-year-old started 5; won 2, second 1, third 1; won $7,430. Third Flamingo Stakes at Hialeah.	50-1	
PICTOR	b. c.	Challenger / Lady Legend	W. L. Brann	Started 3 times as 2-year-old; second 1, third 1; won $280. Won first out as 3-year-old at Bowie.	50-1	
BASHFUL DUCK	br. c.	Chicle / Baba Kenny	E. R. Bradley	As 2-year-old started 2; won 1, third 1; won $790. Wintered at Idle Hour.	40-1	
GRAMPS	b. c.	Equipoise / Kinswoman	J. H. Whitney	As 2-year-old started 3; unplaced in all. Wintered at Columbia, S.C.	60-1	
GENERAL MANAGER	br. c.	Morvich / Agnes Ayres	Mrs. E. G. Lewis	As 2-year-old started 15; won 1, second 3, third 3; won $2,925. Started once as 3-year-old; finished 3rd to older horses.	60-1	
ASP	ch. c.	Diavolo / Nile Maiden	Wheatley Stable	Started 8 times as 2-year-old; won 1, second 1; won $1,255. Wintered at Aqueduct.	50-1	
GALLAHADION	b. c.	Sir Gallahad III / Countess Time	Milky Way Stable (Mrs. Ethel V. Mars)	As 2-year-old started 5 times; second 1; won $180. As 3-year-old started 8 times at Santa Anita; won 3 (one stakes), second 2; won $13,600.	50-1	
SUPER CHIEF	ch. g.	Pot Au Feu / Bourse	Mrs. E. Denemark	As 2-year-old started 2 times; won 1; won $450; As 3-year-old started 5 times; won 1, second 1, third 1; won $3,985. Won Arkansas Derby.	50-1	
DUSKY FOX	b. c.	Display / Flighty Anna	Belair Stud	Started 5 times as 2-year-old; won 1, second 1; won $880. Wintered at Aqueduct.	80-1	
BLACK BRUMMEL	blk. g.	St. James / Reprove	A. L. Ferguson	Started 6 times as 2-year-old; won 2, second 1, third 1; won $2,000. Wintered in Kentucky.	80-1	
MULTITUDE	br. c.	Canaan / Many Thorns	Le Mar Stock Farm	As 2-year-old started 2; won 1, second 1; won $1,275. As 3-year-old started 8; won 1, second 2, third 3; won $2,755.	40-1	
ROYAL MAN	b. c.	Man O'Night / Royal Purple	Tower Stable	As 2-year-old started 3 times; won 1, third 1; won $675. As 3-year-old started 8 times at Hialeah; won 4, second 2; won $4,675.	60-1	
ROBERT E. LEE	br. g.	Quatre Bras II / Annabell Lee	J. F. Byers	As 2-year-old started 6 times, all in England; won 5, second 1; won $5,040.	60-1	
JACOMAR	ch. c.	Jack High / Gay O'Mar	Mrs. E. G. Lewis	As 2-year-old started 11 times; won 3, second 2, third 3; won $4,720. Wintered at Columbia, S.C.	80-1	
CHATTED	ch. c.	Diavolo / Stonechat	Milky Way Farm	As 2-year-old started 11 times; won 4, second 1 third 1; won $2,820. As 3-year-old started 5 times; won 3, second 2; won $3,950. Second Tanforan Derby.	60-1	
GOOD CONDUCT	b. c.	Byrd / Busy Fairy	L. W. Ulmer	As 2-year-old started 5 times; won 2, third 1; won $1,625. Wintered at Douglas Park.	40-1	
ENDY	br. c.	Islam / Peggy Lehmann	Mrs. J. Chesney	As 2-year-old started 18 times; won 3, second 4, third 4; won $2,400. As 3-year-old started 10 times; won 3, second 3, third 2; won $2,425.	60-1	

The following also are possible starters: Alhalon, Ballast Reef, Barnet, Battery, Beauzar, Big Rover, Blue Flyer, Blue Suit, Bonzar, Briar Sharp, Bull Ring, Camban, Cherry Trifle, Cinesar, Clyde Tolson, Connaught, Conscription, Corydon, Count Happy, Designer, Devil Red, Devil's Crag, Displayer, Dollar Bay, Domkin, Ekwanok, Exarch, Flarette, Foxflame, Foxleigh, Gallant Dream, Gino Thor, Golden Per, Gold Teddy, Guerrilla, Happened, Inscolad, Inscolassie, Johnnie J., Kantan, Kayteekeel, King Black, Liberty Franc, Mad Sweep, Maestro Sascha, Marching Sir, McGarvey, Merry Knight, Millbriar, Mission Step, Neb Dorsett, Nightland, Pass Out, Perfect Love, Perfect Rhyme, Philosopher, Pigeon Fly, Predicate, Quenemo, Ramases, Residue, Royal Crusader, Rufigi, Samuel D., Sir Jeffrey, Sir Lancelot, Sky Dog, Snow Ridge, Spanish Main, Stagefright, Star Chance, Star Hunter, St. Croix, Strawberry, Sun Pharos, Supreme Chance, The Rage, Third Covey, Tight Shoes, Tippity, Titilator, Tola Rose, Tough Hombre, Triple Entente, True Star, Valdina Star, Valtite, Votum, White Hunter, Woodvale Lass, Yes or No.

EARLY TIMES

Mrs. Mars was not in attendance at the Derby that year because of ill health. That is why when you see a picture of the winners circle at the Derby Mrs. Mars is not in the picture, she is seen in an inset photo. In 1943 Milky Way Farms entered another horse in the 69th Kentucky Derby. No Wrinkles was slated to be in the field of about ten horses that was to go to post for that event. Unlike Gallahadion, No Wrinkles was widely expected to be a contender that year. However, No Wrinkles did not fare well and was soon only a memory. That's the way it is in the world of horse racing.

May 5,1940

Mrs.Ethel V.Mars
930 Ashland Ave.
River Forest,Ill.

My Dear Mrs.Mars:

I am still so thrilled over the Derby victory I just don't
know what to do.I have never been so happy in all my life
over anything.I am so glad for such a victory because you
surely deserved it,but I am so sorry that you were not able
to see the colors come down in front.You know I just had a
feeling all the time that Gallahadion was going to win the
Derby.I would have given anything to have seen the race I
have always dreamed of being there and seeing the colors
come down in front,although I was not there in person I was
there 100% in heart and no one rooted any harder than I
did and I was just so thrilled I could hardly stand it when
the announcer said Gallahadion was in front and that
Gallahadion was the winner.There were lots of the fellows
that work out on the farm in the office listening to the
race and you should have heard the cheering and rejoicing
when the winner was Gallahadion.Everyone is just thrilled
to death and everyone so happy for you won.

After the race the telephone started ringing and calls were
coming in from all over the county,from Pulaski,from Nashville,
and other places congratulating you on such a great Derby
victory for Giles County and for Tennessee,and for yourself.
I have never seen anything like how people around Pulaski are
excited over the victory.Everyone is just so happy that you
won.

Mrs.Mars I wish you would have Roy send us a picture of

Gallahadion and the finish of the race to hang up in the office for there will be lots of people come by the office and want to see the picture of our Derby winner. I would also like to have a picture of him myself to keep and cherish. But that victory was one of the biggest thrills I have ever gotten in my life.

Everything is going along just fine here on the farms. The weather is getting nice down here. The feeder cattle that Alen purchased were unloaded here on Friday and Saturday. We got them here in good shape and they surely are a nice bunch of cattle.

Mr. Donaldson has been down for the past three weeks and he has been getting the Thoroughbred barn cleaned up and it is in good shape. All the horses here are just fine and the colts are swell.

I am so sorry that you have not been feeling well and I did not know that you were sick until Friday. I surely hope that you are feeling much better and will soon be up and be able to come down and spend quite a bit of time on the farms. We surely have missed your being away so long and are looking forward to your coming and staying a long time with us real soon. I have been thinking of you so much since I learned that you had not been feeling so well and I surely hope that you will be much improved real soon.

Kindly give my best regards to Miss Storck.

With kindest personal regards to you from both Christine, and myself, I am

Most Sincerely,

This is the radio that was used in the office to listen to the Derby by Sam Collins and many other employees.

Sam Collins was one excited human being when Gallahadion won the Kentucky Derby, so were a lot of other people. To win the Derby would put Milky Way Farms on top in thoroughbred circles. This letter on the previous page talks about many employees of the farm being in the office listening to the race with Sam Collins on the radio. I have the zenith radio that they listened to in my office today. By the standards of today a radio doesn't seem like a big deal but in a rural county where there were still a lot of people who did not have electricity it was a luxury.

This Zenith radio was in the store at Milky Way Farms. Many people came to the store just to be able to listen to the radio. Times have changed, haven't they? I have this radio in my collection also.

Gallahadion.

This is one of the shoes worn by Gallahadion the day that he won the Kentucky Derby. The statement of provenance in the middle of the shoe is signed by your author. This shoe was the one that was on display in the office.

Roy Waldron, the Milky Way Farms race horse trainer at his stable in California.

HONOR ROLL OF MILKY WAY FARMS THOROUGHBRED HORSES

TIGER	Winner—Arlington Park Futurity (Dead Heat), Washington Park Futurity Arkansas Derby. Second—Belmont Futurity.
FOREVER YOURS	Winner—Lassie Stakes, Spinaway Stakes.
CASE ACE	Winner—Arlington Futurity, Illinois Derby.
REAPING REWARD	Winner—Latonia Derby, New England Futurity, Kentucky Jockey Club Stakes, United States Hotel Stakes. Third—Kentucky Derby.
MARS SHIELD	Winner—Texas Derby, Kentucky Oaks.
WELL REWARDED	Winner—Princess Pat Stakes.
SKY LARKING	Winner—Hopeful Stakes, Bashford Manor Stakes, Albany Handicap.
SANGREAL	Winner—Albany Handicap.
GALLAHADION	Winner—Kentucky Derby, San Vicente Handicap. Second—Arlington Classic Stakes. Third—Preakness Stakes.
MOUNTAIN RIDGE	Winner—Kentucky Jockey Club Stakes, Steger Handicap.
UP THE CREEK	Winner—Clark Handicap.
BLACK RAIDER	Winner—Bashford Manor Stakes, Saratoga Sales Stakes, Lafayette Stakes, Santa Barbara Stakes.
DOGPATCH	Winner—Futurity Trial.
TALMA DEE	Winner—Selima Stakes.
NO COMPETITION	Winner—Grand Union Hotel Stakes. Second—Arlington Futurity, Yerba Buena Handicap.
DOGAWAY	Winner—Juvenile Stakes, Hawthorne Juvenile Handicap.
WHISKOLO	Winner—Ivanhoe Club Handicap. Second—Santa Anita Derby. Second— Texas Derby. Third—Kentucky Derby.
MURPH	Winner—Bashford Manor Stakes.
DINNER DATE	Winner—Spinaway Stakes, Matron Stakes.
THE FIGHTER	Winner—Texas Derby, Grand Union Hotel Stakes, Remsen Handicap, Inaugural Handicap, Blue Bonnet Handicap.

This honor roll of thoroughbred horses was featured in the farm brochure.

MARS *Incorporated*

2019 to 2059 North Oak Park Ave.
Chicago, Illinois

July 6, 1940

Mr. S. T. Collins, Jr.,
Milky Way Farms,
Pulaski, Tenn.

Dear Sam:

I expect some friends of mine, Mr. and
Mrs. Elmer Hassman, to stop at the Farms some time between
July 20th and 27th. They have been south on a vacation and
are planning on returning to Chicago by way of Nashville
so I asked them to stop at the Farms and that you or someone else would be glad to show them around.

I would very much appreciate your per-
sonally showing them around the Farms, if you are not too
busy. In case you are absent or busy would you have someone else take them around.

With kindest regards, I am

Yours truly,

G. B. Hurley

GBH*VG

This was one of the perks of being a member of the Mars Inc. family. You could use Milky Way Farms as
a place for your friends to go and spend as much time as they liked.

HOME OF
REGISTERED HEREFORD CATTLE
THOROUGHBRED HORSES

PULASKI, TENNESSEE

January 16,1941

Mrs.Ethel V.Mars
Huntington Hotel
Pasadena,California

My Dear Mrs.Mars:

How are you feeling ? Surely hope you are feeling fine.I know you must
be enjoying the wonderful California weather.The weather has been nice
here ever since the first of January.The sun has shone most everyday.It
has rained today for the first time.Surely is a contrast between this
January and last January.This time last year there was a big snow on
the ground here.Guess we will be getting our share of the bad weather
soon though.

How are all the race horses doing.Surely was sorry to see Black Raider
lose those two ra ces.Looks like he might be a pretty good colt.How are
all the yearlings doing.I don't hear much news about the horses except
what I read in the Form.Surely hope that After Dawn trains good for the
Derby and I am pulling for him to win it.Which of the yearlings do you
think will be the best out there on the coast.You see I want a tip so
I can win a bet on one of them.Ha Ha How is Gallahadion training and do
you think he will be ready for the big race.How is Roy getting along?Hope
he is fine.

Everything is mighty quite around here since evryone has gone away.Surely
do miss everyone.I amagine that Mr.& Mrs.Feeney are enjoying the Arizona
climate.I surely would like to see the West it must be nice out there.
Abraham and I are keeping each other company and we talk about you all nearly
every day.It is so quite here we get lonesome for some of the family.
Abe is getting a rest and is enjoying it.He asks me nearly evry day if I
have heard from you and how you are getting along.

The farm is just fine and things are running real smooth and nice.I have
sold two bulls since Alan left.Sold one for $200.00 and one for $275.00.
Have two or three other good prospects.I have bought about 100 hogs and
put in the feed lot behind the 172 steers that we have on feed.Hogs have
gone up quite a bit since I bought them.The market has advanced about 2¢
per pound.Hope it stays up until about June if it does we will do awfully

HOME OF
REGISTERED HEREFORD CATTLE
THOROUGHBRED HORSES

PULASKI, TENNESSEE

The steers that we have on feed are doing good.I have bought about
25,000 bushels of corn and have it in the crib.The corn market has advanced
about 5¢ per bushel since we bought our requirement.Our corn cost us 60¢
per bushel put in the crib.Think it was a real good buy.I am doing quite
a bit of cleaning up around the garage and places that need it this winter.
I want to have everything looking good when Alan comes back and you get
back in the spring.Mrs.Mars I am certainly trying to do the very best that
I can do to make the farm look good and save money on things.I surely
would appreciate your telling me if I am not doing all that I should do.
I have tried hard to do the very best possible and I know that I have made
some mistakes but I promise that I will not make the same mistake twice.
You don't know I do appreciate the confidence that you have placed in me
and I assure you that I will always do the very best in my power.

I have had to send in my Selective Service questionaire and the local board
has advised me that I have been placed in Third class.So I don't guess I
will have to go to training camp for three or four years anyway.Maybe by
then everything will be settled.I have been elected President of the Pulaski
Exchange Club for the coming year.The Club is composed of about 50 business
men of Pulaski.I feel quite honored by being selected and I going to do my
best to make a good one and be helpful to the Club. I have also been elected
a member of the Junior Chamber of Commerce.

Christine is just doing fine.

Give my best regards to Miss Quinlan and with kindest personal regards to
you,I am

Most Sincerely,

This letter gives the reader an idea of what was going on at the farm and in the life of Sam Collins.
Notice the change of personal secretary from Storcky to Miss Quinlin.

HOME OF
REGISTERED HEREFORD CATTLE
THOROUGHBRED HORSES

Pulaski, Tennessee

Huntington Hotel
Pasadena, Calfornia
January 20, 1941

Mr. S. H. Collins
Milky Way Farms
Pulaski, Tenn.

My dear Sam:

I was very pleased to receive your letter of January 16th and note how
well things are going at the Farm. I have no complaint as to the way you
are handling your work and no suggestions to make at this time.

First I wish to tell you that I am feeling fine and putting on weight.
We have had delightful weather the past week. Previously there was some
rain.

By this time you will know that we had to destroy After Dawn, which was indeed a great shock to all of us. He was the best three year old prospect
we had and was entered in all of the big stakes. I am hoping that one or
two of the others will develope so we can run them. It is hard for me to
tell you which of the two year olds we consider the best. We have many,
which we think are good. Black Raider shows plenty of speed and we think
will go a fair distance. Signal Flash will be a splendid colt, but we are
not pushing him as he ought to make an outstanding three year old. Stepsome
is coming along very rapidly and we expect to run him this Friday. The
fillies, My Choice, Laila Brooks are doing very well - although neither one
has been started. Gallahadion has not been very well, but is much better and
Roy is now training him. I cannot predict how he will come out in the Handicap if he is able to start. It will be a very tough race with very strong
competition.

I am sure it must be very lonesome there with all of us gone. Please tell
Abraham that I will write him very soon and that I appreciated his letter.
I am glad that you were placed in third class of the selective service. I
don't believe that you will have to worry about having to go for some time
to come. I congratulate you on being elected President of the Pulaski Exchange Club. That is a great honor for one of your age.

Write me whenever you have the urge Sam, as I am always glad to hear from
you. With kindest personal regards to all, I am

Sincerely,

ETHEL V. MARS

EVM:Q

Did you wonder what happened to Gallahadion after he won the derby? Well, as you can see, he was
still training but was not doing very well. Mrs. Mars also congratulated Sam Collins for being elected the
president of the Exchange Club in Pulaski.

ETHEL V. MARS

930 ASHLAND AVENUE	MARLANDS	MILKY WAY FARMS
RIVER FOREST	MINOCQUA	PULASKI
ILLINOIS	WISCONSIN	TENNESSEE

Marlands,
Minocqua, Wisconsin
July 15, 1941

Mr. Sam Collins, Jr.
Milky Way Farms
Pulaski, Tenn.

My dear Sam:

First allow me to congratulate you on your wonderful new
baby girl and to tell you how happy I am that she and
Christine are doing nicely. I can hardly wait to see them.

I am glad you like your new Ford Coupe and hope you will
take very good care of it as I do not know when you will
get another new car.

We have all had a very lovely time at Marlands and I was
sorry to see Patty and the Children go home Sunday night.
I shall, of course, leave about the first of August for
Saratoga and will be gone all of that month, but I plan
on coming down to the Farm sometime during September.

Alan says you have had nice rains and that the pastures
are in excellent condition. He was also very enthusiastic
about the purchase of the show herd. He seems to feel that
we have all the tops for any show this year.

I like the stationery very much and want to thank you for
sending me some. Do not forget that you are going to take
a little vacation and come to Saratoga during the month of
August. Let no one talk you out of this.

With kindest personal regards, I am

Sincerely,

Ethel V. Mars

ETHEL V. MARS

EVM:Q

Mrs. Mars was congratulating Sam Collins on the birth of my sister and telling him she wanted him to come to Saratoga during August.

This was the new stationery that Mrs. Mars was making reference too.

Pulaski, Tenn., July 18, 1941 ....194.........

M............ Mrs. Sam Collins

Milky Way Farm--Pulaski, Tennessee

In Account With

PULASKI HOSPITAL

DR. W. J. JOHNSON — DR. J. U. SPEER

Telephone 140

ALL HOSPITAL ACCOUNTS PAYABLE IN ADVANCE

405 E. Jefferson St.

Hospital Bill........ ....$25.00
Special Nurse Board Bill..... .... 4.00
                    Total charge...........$29.00

Paid 7/18/46

Pulaski Hospital
J. U. Speer M.D.

This has absolutely nothing to do with the history of Milky Way Farms but I just thought you might want to see what the hospital bill was for my sister's birth. Times have changed a little haven't they?

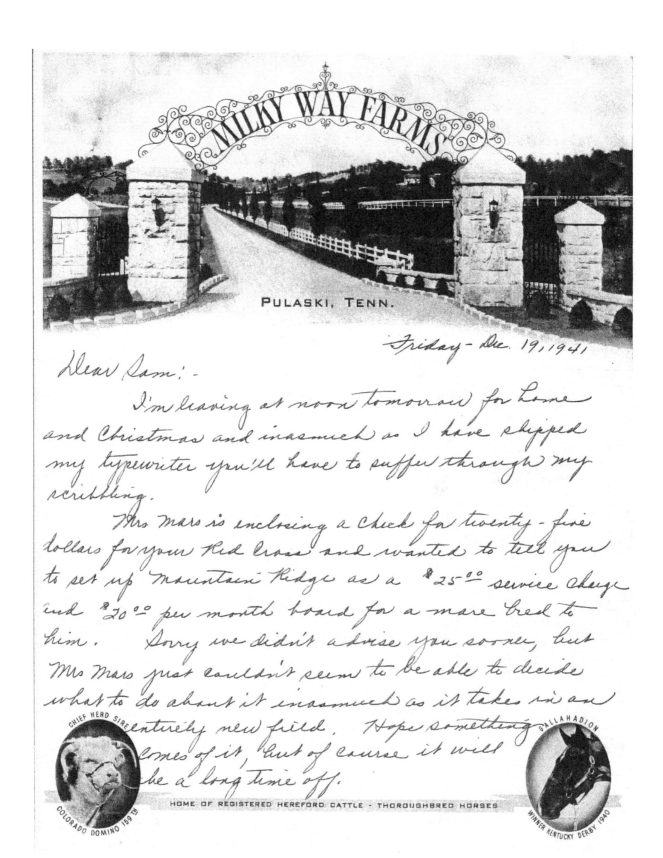

MILKY WAY FARMS

PULASKI, TENN.

Friday - Dec. 19, 1941

Dear Sam: -

I'm leaving at noon tomorrow for home and Christmas and inasmuch as I have shipped my typewriter you'll have to suffer through my scribbling.

Mrs Mars is enclosing a check for twenty-five dollars for your Red Cross and wanted to tell you to set up "Mountain Ridge" as a $25.00 service charge and $20.00 per month board for a mare bred to him. Sorry we didn't advise you sooner, but Mrs Mars just couldn't seem to be able to decide what to do about it inasmuch as it takes in an entirely new field. Hope something comes of it, but of course it will be a long time off.

CHIEF HERD SIRE

COLORADO DOMINO 159 TH

GALLAHADION

WINNER KENTUCKY DERBY 1940

HOME OF REGISTERED HEREFORD CATTLE - THOROUGHBRED HORSES

I certainly wish you all the success in the world as Chairman of the Red Cross. I mean to join some unit of its service when I come back, after the first of the year. Don't know whether you know, or not, but we are not going to California this year. Patty has persuaded her mother to spend the winter here and with the racing uncertain on the West Coast and general conditions as they are it is probably best. We may go out the latter part of February for a few weeks.

Well Sam - guess thats all for now - My very best wishes to you, your wife and little girl for a very happy Christmas.

Sincerely,

Marie Quinlan

This hand written letter from Marie Quinlin gives you the feeling that things had changed for a lot of people and the beginning of the Second World War would change everybody's life. Nothing would be the same again.

It is largely believed in the community that Mrs. Mars built the Catholic Church that stood next to the First Baptist Church on South First Street in Pulaski. That original building is now the Trail of Tears Interpretive Center near Sam Davis Park. She did not fund the entire project but had it not been for her generous donation in honor of her late husband it would not have been built. The Pulaski Citizen had this to say about the new church in August of 1941. "The new Catholic Church on South First Street which was completed this week is the latest addition to Pulaski's large number of churches. The building, which was started several months ago through a magnificent gift of Mrs. Ethel V. Mars and her daughter, Mrs. Alan Feeney, is a memorial to the late Frank C. Mars, who came to Giles County ten years ago, where he established the famous Milky Way Farms. Mr. Mars died in 1934 and is buried on a high hill overlooking the farm. This beautiful chapel, of the Gothic type of architecture , is constructed of native limestone approximately 30 X 65 feet, at a cost of $5,000. The old church, St. Augustine located on South Fourth Street has been purchased by the city." I am not trying to diminish Mrs. Mars' gift that made the church a reality but merely trying to make sure that the record is correct.

3-11-4²

Dear Sam —

I am enclosing a list of
a few more names for booklets to be sent to.

We are nearly out of meat here so
it would be well to have some butchering
done and then send the meat a week from
Friday — Have them kill a hog, 9 lamb & a
steer.

I am leaving here Monday morning
taking Eastern to Atlanta and then Delta
Airlines to Ft. Worth. Will be in Ft. Worth
at Worth Hotel Monday night and for
following 2 or 3 days. I don't know
just when I will be back to Tenn. as I may
try to buy some more cows or heifers before
coming home. I will let you know

of my whereabouts if I am to be anywhere for any length of time and will notify you when to have Harry meet me.

I am pleased to see those hogs make some money. We have put quite a lot in them though and they would certainly have been a poor investment if the market had gone off two or three dollars a cwt.

Mrs Mens and I have talked the horse situation over and she is in favor of selling several of them and buying a few good cowhorses. So when they begin to look good on spring grass we may dispose of 8 or 10 for whatever they will bring.

Regards
Alan

This hand written letter from Alan Feeney gives the reader a little insight into how he fit into the operation of the farm.

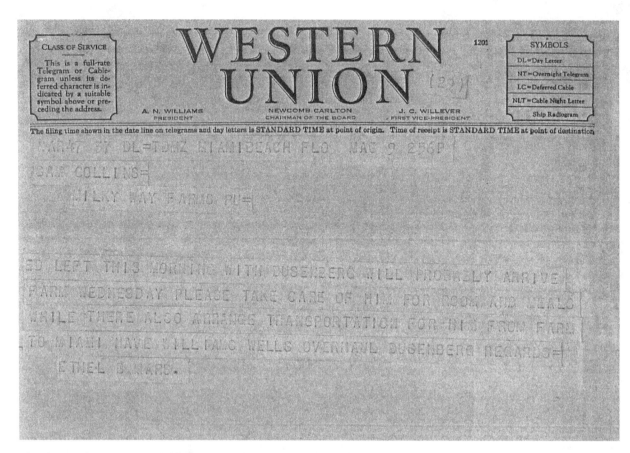

The duesenberg automobile was one of the more expensive sold in America. Would you expect that William Wells would be allowed to overhaul such an auto in the garage at Milky Way Farms? Harvey Dickey and William Wells both worked on it and drove it to Chicago and other destinations.   Harvey Dickey's sons, Larry and Dean Dickey have close ties to Milky Way Farms.

PULASKI, TENN.

6020 N. Bay Road
Miami Beach, Fla.
March 24, 1942

Mr. Sam Collins
Milky Way Farms
Pulaski, Tenn.

My dear Sam:

I am enclosing a list of names for the distribution of the Milky Way booklets, as Alan suggested. I understand you will go over the list to be sure there are no duplications.

You asked me in your letter about Roy and the shipping of the horses. You perhaps know by now what has happened. At any rate, Roy shipped out last Sunday and expects to arrive in Lexington tomorrow, Wednesday. He intends to send "Deserving" and "Educated" to the Farm. He said all of the other horses were doing very well, but that "Gallahadion" could not train on account of his leg. I am planning to leave him at Mr. Knight's place for a while and breed him to the mares, which I have transferred there from Mr. Thomas' Farm.

We have been solicited for a donation to the maintenance of Martin College and I feel that we should make a contribution. The Farm means a great deal to the people in that community and I have decided to give them $1,000.00 (one thousand dollars). I have already made a personal contribution to them as I think it would be a shame to close the school after it has been in existence since the Civil war. You can handle this through the customary channels.

I presume Alan has arrived there and while he planned on coming back to have his knee attended to I doubt very much whether he will do so. We are leaving here April 9th and will stop off at Lexington for about a week. I am anxious to see Roy.

HOME OF REGISTERED HEREFORD CATTLE - THOROUGHBRED HORSES

PULASKI, TENN.

(Sam Collins - 2 -)

and also look over the horses.

Patty certainly has a pretty little baby and we are all thrilled that we have
another little girl. The baby is gaining very rapidly and both she and Patty
are feeling fine.

Thanks for looking after Ed so nicely while at the Farm and assure William
Wells that there is no particular rush in fixing the Duesenberg. I may have
to have him drive it to Chicago, but will let you know about that later on.
Ed says your little girl is as cute as can be and he got a great kick out of
her. I am sure she must be a good deal of company for you and Christine as
well as a joy.

With kindest regards to you all, I am

                                            Sincerely,

                                            Ethel V. Mars

                                            ETHEL V. MARS

EVM:Q

HOME OF REGISTERED HEREFORD CATTLE · THOROUGHBRED HORSES

Gallahadion was injured and his recovery was doubtful. Mrs. Mars shows that she was a real benefit to
the community by donating to Martin College and there was no rush on fixing the Duesenberg.

PULASKI, TENNESSEE

The booklet that Mrs. Mars is making reference to in the letter of March 24, 1942. This booklet was sent to special guests and given to those who came to the farm for a tour. Remember the directions of Mr. Hoben to Sam Collins about the friends of his who he wanted to be treated well at the farm. They would have gotten a booklet.

The envelope that the booklet was stored in.

September 5,1942

Mrs.Ethel V.Mars
930 Ashland Ave.
River Forest,Ill.

My Dear Mrs.Mars:

I haven't heard from you lately and were just wondering how
you were feeling.I surely hope that you are feeling much
better by now.

We are busy putting up hay now.We surely have lots of it to
put up and it is real nice.We have had some wonderful rains
and the pastures and everything look mighty good now.

I haven't been able to find anyone around here to break the
three yearlings that we have here at the farms.Roy said that
he couldn't get any boys to come down to the farm and for me
to try and pick up a kid around here but so far I have been
unable to find one but am still looking and trying to get hold
of a boy.All the horses are looking good and doing fine.

When are you coming down?I hope you will be able to get down
and stay a long time with us this fall.

   With kindest personal regards,I am

                Sincerely,

I am sure that by now you have noticed that Sam Collins asked frequently how Mrs. Mars health was
when he wrote to her. You have also noticed that Mrs. Mars was not spending much time at the farm.
Both of these things are indications of bad things to come.

~~February~~ March 4, 1943

Dear Sam –

I am enclosing expense account and my check for $106 –

We have our reservations to leave here March 24th 10:00 A.m. – Arrive Nashville about 11:30 A.m. 25th. Colored help will want to leave here 24th also – So I expect William Wells had better plan to arrive here March 22nd in order to have the 23rd to work on Oldsmobile. Mrs. Fleming will stay a day or two after we leave to close up the house and William can stay and bring her back with him in Lincoln.

We will want both Abraham and Harvey to meet us in Nashville with the Cadillac + De Soto. Probably want a truck to go into Nashville after trunks we will check – about 26th

I don't recall whether or not I talked with you about getting the dead shrubbery replaced.

I imagine it would be well to have Trischler do the work as soon as possible. Or as there may not be such a large amount you may be able to buy from someone close to Milky Way Farms. All dead or dying trees along entrance road should be replaced with Chinese elms — other plants can be replaced with whatever variety was used previously.

Regarding Jarry coming 5th. If we hear nothing from Mr. Bidwell — I believe I would plan on truck being ready to leave Bidwell ranch with bull on March 17th.

Roy is shipping to Louisville march 22nd. He may send one or two to farm from there. No Wrinkles looks and acts like an nice 3 year old. I believe the two cohorts are about the best 2 year old colts just now. The Foray II filly looked real good.

Everyone is well here and all anxious to get home — especially me.

Hoping all grand well and with best regards

A. F.

Alan Feeney didn't have many letters typed. Notice the instructions he gave to have Abraham Macklin and Harvey Dickey to meet them in Nashville with the Cadillac and Desoto.

ETHEL V. MARS

930 ASHLAND AVENUE	MARLANDS	MILKY WAY FARMS
RIVER FOREST	MINOCQUA	PULASKI
ILLINOIS	WISCONSIN	TENNESSEE

July 10, 1943

Dear Sam:

Enclosed is Mrs. Mars' check for bets. She said that she
may owe you more, as she had told Alan to bet on - I believe
it was Red Wonder the time she ran before she won. If she
does owe you anymore just let us know and we'll send a check.

Sorry I didn't get down to the Farm with Mrs. Mars, but I
didn't think she would stay so long. Would have liked to see
you all again.

Roy has gotten rid of most of the horses now. He sold Educated
yesterday, Lady Ruler last Saturday and Riskton was claimed
during last week. Won't be long now.

Hope to see you this Fall.

Best regards,

Marie Quinlan

Remember that Marie Quinlan was Mrs. Mars personal secretary and had her finger on the pulse of
what was taking place. Just a short while ago you were told that bad things were about to happen.
Well, the race horses were being sold and as Marie Quinlan stated, "Won't be long now".

BIGELOW 3-7310

MARS AND HUZENLAUB

~~211 BROAD AVENUE~~
~~NEWARK, NEW JERSEY~~
2001 Nance Street
Houston 10, Texas
December 14, 1943

Mr. Sam Collins
Milky Way Farms
Pulaski, Tennessee

Dear Sam:

I am sending you some of our "converted" rice, which I hope you will like. Please distribute it among the employees.

Kindest regards.

Yours sincerely,

F E Mars

FEMars:jd

As we have already discussed, Forrest Mars was not in the picture in the formation of Milky Way Farms. He wanted his father's horse and nothing else. He had introduced M&M candies and was now introducing converted rice. Later he would be in charge of Mars Inc. He was sending a shipment of this new product to the employees at Milky Way to get their reaction.

156

march 7,1944

Mrs.Ethel V.Mars
R#7 Box 466
Phoenix,Arizona

My Dear Mrs.Mars:

We had quite an electrical storm here yesterday and lightning
struck #5 Barn or you might remember it as the "Barn of Many
Gables" and burned it up.We had about 40 tons of grass hay in
the barn that we had cut off the farm.There was no other loss
just the barn and hay.We surely have been having lots of rain
the past month.The creek has been out over the bottoms three
or four times lately.Grass is coming out fine and is looking
good.If we don't have any more freezes we should be able to
turn out on grass quite a bit earlier this year.

I have had the four tires on your car recapped.The extra did
not need recapping.Sure got some good rubber put on them and
a real job of recapping.The cost was $8.15 each making a total
of $32.60.

Hope that you are feeling just fine and enjoying the climate
there.

With kindest personal regards, I am

                    Sincerely,

This was the second barn to burn. It was known as the "barn of many gables". The first barn to burn
was filled with straw.

PULASKI, TENN.

Phoenix, Arizona
March 11, 1944

Mr. Sam Collins, Jr.
Milky Way Farms
Pulaski, Tenn.

My dear Sam:

I received your letter this morning and was certainly sorry to hear about the No. 5
barn burning. This is the second barn we have lost in that manner, both of which
was filled with hay and straw. This is quite a loss to us as we have no insurance.

Roy wrote me you had quite a lot of rain and that the bottoms were overflowing. As
you say, it may be a great help to the grass, which is some consolation.

Thanks for having my tires recapped. I am enclosing my check for the charges of
$32.60, which amount I think is very reasonable. I am also enclosing check for
$100.00 as my contribution to your Red Cross drive.

I am feeling well and am thoroughly enjoying the weather out here, which at this
time is particularly nice. We have been having sunny days and cool nights. It has
been very quiet as we go out seldom, but we get lots of rest and that is the main
thing. However, I will be very glad to get back home and expect to leave here about
April 15th and go by way of the Farm.

I am so glad Sam that you will continue to be with us. I can assure you it is a
great relief. Hoping everything is going along smoothly, I am with kindest personal
regards

Sincerely,

Ethel V. Mars

ETHEL V. MARS

EVM:Q

HOME OF REGISTERED HEREFORD CATTLE - THOROUGHBRED HORSES

Did you find it strange that Milky Way Farms did not have insurance on the No. 5 barn? Some people
carried their own insurance.

April 8, 1944

Mrs. Ethel V. Mars
R#7 Box 466
Phoenix, Arizona

My Dear Mrs. Mars:

The flowers for Mr. Mars grave arrived in good condition
and were very beautiful. We placed them on the grave upon
arrival.

We are surely having lots of rain here. Everything looks mighty
green and pretty.

I suppose that you will be coming here shortly.

With kindest personal regards, I am

                    Sincerely,

Remember this was the tenth year anniversary of Mr. Mars death. Mr. Mars body was still on the farm
and the mausoleum would be moved later that year.

Before the announcement of the sale of the farm Mrs. Mars had instructed Sam Collins to come up with a list of the proposed reimbursement to Milky Way Farms employees. Mrs. Mars had promised the employees that had been loyal that she would give them severance compensation.

MARS Incorporated

2019 to 2059 North Oak Park Ave.
Chicago 35, Illinois

August 30, 1944

Mr. S. T. Collins, Jr.
Milky Way Farms
Pulaski, Tennessee

Dear Sam:

We are enclosing herewith a list of the proposed reimbursement to Milky Way Farms employees, which is effective upon the final disposal of the farm. It is understood, of course, that they will have to stay at their regular salaries until the farm is disposed of in order to obtain this additional compensation. We believe that the employees concerned should now be told and we believe that most of them will stay with the farm until the disposal has been effected.

We received the map and your letter yesterday. With best regards, we are

Very truly yours,

MARS, INCORPORATED

G. B. Hurley
Treasurer

GBH:emd
enc.

"When you crave good candy — Milky Way"

MARS *Incorporated*

2019 to 2059 North Oak Park Ave.,
Chicago 35, Illinois

April 25, 1945

Mr. S. T. Collins, Jr.
Milky Way Farms
Pulaski, Tennessee

Dear Sam:

We are enclosing herewith list of Milky Way Farms employees for severance pay. You will note that we have shown the approved bonus, the proposed, and the amounts where approval was less than Mrs. Mars had promised the employees. In all of the other cases, the approval is more than the proposed.

Will you kindly go over this list and tell us just what you think of it and how it is best to handle. Best regards,

Very truly yours,

MARS, INCORPORATED

G. B. Hurley
Financial Director and
Treasurer

GBH:emd
enc.

"When you crave good candy — Milky Way"

161

MILKY WAY FARMS - SEVERANCE PAY

	APPROVED	PROPOSED	APPROVED LESS THAN PROPOSED
S. T. Collins, Jr.	-3,120.00	10,000.00	6,880.00
Frank T. Thurman	-2,400.00	2,200.00	
Brown Hardiman	-1,684.80	1,650.00	
Henry Davis	-967.20	500.00	
Thurman Deason	-470.40	300.00	
Alan Francis	-47.12	150.00	102.88
Floyd Macklin	-59.86	250.00	190.14
Bud Gardner	-215.28	250.00	34.72
Patrick Gardner	-430.56	250.00	
Pete Graves	-1,339.20	2,200.00	860.80
Harvey Dickey	-595.20	600.00	4.80
Rufus Lawhorn	-48.00	100.00	52.00
Sherman Gilliam	-1,747.20	2,000.00	252.80
Willaim Wells	-2,203.20	1,500.00	
Russell Woodard	-921.60	300.00	
Tommy Tarpley	-240.00	300.00	60.00
Horace Woodard	-288.58	300.00	11.42
William O'Neal	-2,217.60	2,000.00	
Ed Martin	-654.12	250.00	
Rossie Butler	-540.00	250.00	
Mrs. Aileen Fleming	-780.00	1,000.00	220.00
Lena Martin	-518.40	500.00	
Vernell Morris	-259.20	250.00	
Lizzie Tally	-117.04	100.00	
Lizzie Gardner	-172.80	100.00	
Ed McNeese	-991.76	1,500.00	508.24
Shelly Story	-998.40	1,500.00	501.60
Josh Wright	-130.30	250.00	119.70
Porter Martin	-394.40	250.00	
Marvin Martin	-203.04	500.00	296.96
Willie Fralix	-240.00	250.00	10.00
Cecil Gilliam	-288.00	300.00	12.00
LeeRoy Macklin	-776.88	250.00	
Waymon Harwell	-273.00	500.00	227.00
Robert McMillen	-119.72	100.00	
Mark Carpenter	-72.00	100.00	28.00
Jim Jones	-108.32	100.00	
Andy Gordon	-796.32	250.00	
Dave Pullen	-50.24	100.00	49.76
Charles Goodwin	-987.84	600.00	
Jesse Wright	-480.00	300.00	
Roy Waldron	1,872.00	2,000.00	

3,542.82
6,880.00
10,422.82

You know that Sam Collins made the list out. He thought a great deal of his importance. You also notice that Mr. Hurley did not concur with that assessment. He will get what he asked for a little later. That

will be part of the continuing story. Abraham Macklin was the only employee to get a pension for life.
He got $50.00 a month for life.

September 13,1944

Mr.H.H.Hoben
Mars Inc.
Chicago,Ill.

Dear Mr.Hoben:

I am enclosing herewith a copy of the appraisal as made by
the men on last Monday.They are also forwarding you a copy
but I thought you might like another one also.

I think that they have everything in line very well.I believe
that the club house should have been a little higher because
there is some valuable furniture in it and it cost quite a
bit to build that house also.The swimming pool looks like it
is in a little low.

I presume that you will change some of the figures anyway in
preparing your prospectus.

With kindest regards,I am

Sincerely,

Sam Collins letter to Mr. Hoben refers to the appraisal made by Erskrine Sharp, Thurman Smith and
Herbert Smith.

APPRAISAL MILKY WAY FARMS BY COMMITTEE COMPOSED OF--

THURMAN SMITH--ERSKINE SHARP--HERBERT SMITH

SEPTEMBER 11, 1944

1000 Acres Land @ $200.00 per acre---------$200,000.00
1705 Acres Land @ $100.00 per acre--------- 170,500.00
                                            $370,500.00 $370,500.00

<u>Buildings</u>

#1 Barn	1,000.00	
#2 Feeder Barn & Scales in Feed Lot	5,000.00	
#3 Slaughter House	250.00	
#4 Corn crib-feed mill-shuck house and machinery	15,000.00	
#5 Sheep Barn	1,500.00	
#6 Feed Barn Grindstone Hollow	5,000.00	
#7 Show cattle barn-	7,500.00	
#8 Colt Barn-34 Stalls 487x45	15,000.00	
#9 Garage Building 290x75	5,000.00	
#10 Hay Barn	5,000.00	
#11 Barn	500.00	
#12 Dairy Barn and equipment	7,500.00	
#13 Blacksmith Shop	2,500.00	
#14 Mule Barn 18 Stalls	7,500.00	
#15 Plantation Barn	1,500.00	
#16 Oat House and Equipment	2,500.00	
#17 Stud Barn	3,500.00	
#18 Horse Barn	2,000.00	
#19 Horse Barn	2,000.00	
#20 Horse Barn	2,000.00	
#21 Horse Barn	2,000.00	
#22 Tack House	1,500.00	
#23 Tack House	1,500.00	
#24 Stone Barn 300x50	3,000.00	
#25 Stone Barn 210x60	2,000.00	
#26 Stone Barn 300x50	5,000.00	
#27 Crooked Barn	3,000.00	
#28 Hereford Sales Barn	7,500.00	
#29 Race Horse Barn 250x75-24 Stalls and race track in connection	20,000.00	138,000.00
	$137,250.00	137,250.00

1 Hay Shed for Feeding Dairy Cows --- 750.00
                                      136,750.00

Trench Silo   1,000.00   1,000.00

Rock Crusher   500.00

2 Sets Fairbanks-Morse Truck Scales
  20 Ton Capacity @ $1,000.00 each   2,000.00   2,000.00

Houses & Cottages

Simmons House	$5,000.00	
Hogan House	5,000.00	
15 Cottages 4 Rooms-Bath & Porch	22,500.00	
17 Cottages-Negro-2 and 3 rooms	8,500.00	
5 Cottages-Whites-2 and 3 rooms	2,500.00	
3 Cottages -Collins-Graves and Thurman	9,000.00	
1 Managers Residence	6,000.00	
1 Servants House	1,500.00	
1 House-Hardiman	2,500.00	
1 House-Rhea	3,500.00	
1 House-Oneal	3,000.00	
Club House-Furnishings-Heating and Refrigeration	100,000.00	
	$167,000.00	$167,000.00
Green House	250.00	250.00
Office Building	3,000.00	3,000.00
Swimming Pool and Tennis Court and Equipment	10,000.00	10,000.00
35 Miles Plank Fencing Aprox.277,200 Ft @ $3.00	8,316.00	~~xtyxkkxxx~~0
4000 Concrete Post @ $1.00	4,000.00	
14,480 Locust Post @ 25¢	3,620.00	
	15,936.00	15,936.00
Aprox.20 Miles Roads-Paved and Gravel and Bridges	12,500.00	12,500.00
5½ Miles Electric Lines	3,850.00	
21 5 KW Transformers	1,547.49	
6 10 KW Transformers	721.20	
2 15 KW Transformers	290.84	
6 25 KW Transformers	1,345.08	
	7,754.61	7,754.61
2½ Miles 4" Water Line	9,900.00	
1½ Miles 2" Water Line	3,564.00	
1½ Miles 2½" Water Line	4,356.00	
2 Miles 1" Water Line	3,696.00	
	21,516.00	21,516.00
8 Electric Pumps-Various Sizes	1,200.00	1,200.00

Second page of Sep. 11, 1944 appraisal.

Electric Motors

1 50 H.P. 220 Volt Motor	400.00
1 40 H.P. 220 Volt Motor	322.00
1 30 H.P. 2300 Volt Motor	425.00
2 20 H.P. 220 Volt Motors	320.00
2 10 H.P. 220 Volt Motors	236.00
2 7½ H.P. 220 Volt Motors	184.00
3 5 H.P. 220 Volt Motors	201.00
3 3 H.P. 220 Volt Motors	165.00
10 1 H.P. Motors	300.00
10 ½ to 1 H.P. Motors	300.00
	2953.00

		2,953.00
Water Plant-Filters-Chlorinator-Reservoir-Fire Hydrants and hose	15,000.00	15,000.00
Aprox.320 Tons Coal	1,324.54	1,324.54
Cattle Dipping Vat	750.00	750.00
Miscellaneous Farm equipment, Autos-trucks-tractors,etc.,as per list submitted by Collins	45,894.70	45,894.70
61 Hogs	1,400.00	1,400.00
11 Feeder Cattle	1,250.00	1,250.00
24 Lambs	120.00	120.00

Holstein Cattle

98 Holstein Cows — 86 Cows	12,000.00 10,750.00	
31 Bred Heifers — 21 Bred Heifers 75=	1,860.00 1575.00	
37 Heifers and Yearlings	1,850.00 1850.00	
3 Bulls	450.00 1115.00	
26 Suckling calves go with cows	840.00 910.00	
36	17,000.00 16070.00	17,000.00
9 Mules	1,350.00	1,350.00
24 Horses — 10 Hd.@ $150.00ea 14 Hd. @300.00	2,300.00	2,300.00
		$839,748.55

Third page of Sep. 11, 1944 appraisal.

October 24,1944

Mr.H.H.Hoben
Mars Inc.
2019 N.Oak Park Ave.
Chicago,36
Illinois

Dear Mr.Hoben:

I am enclosing herewith a revised list of equipment and
farm supplies.You will note that I have left off the items
that Mrs.Mars instructed me to leave off in the way of cars
and trucks and also have revised the list and left off some
things that will be taken by Mr.Feeny and you can see the
change in the list by checking this list against the one I
sent you some time ago.Also you will note that Mr.Feeney and
I have revalued some of the items as well as added a few
that had been overlooked.

I imagine that there will be some questions that you will
want to ask me concerning lists and if I can explain any
of the items I will be glad for you to call me and I will go
over the list with you and maybe make it clearer.

With kindest regards,I am

                    Sincerely,

This revised appraisal was done by the same three men that did the first one. The reason it was revised
was the fact that Mrs. Mars decided she did not want some items on the original list to go with the farm.

	Land		$370,500.00
	Building as per appraisal	137250.00	
	Plus 1 Hay Shed left off appraisal	750.00	
		138000.00	138,000.00
	Trench Silo		1,000.00
	Rock Crusher		500.00
	2 Sets Fairbanks-Morse Scales		2,000.00
	Houses and Cottages		167,000.00
	Green House		250.00
	Office Building		3,000.00
	Swimming Pool and Tennis Court		10,000.00
	Concrete and Locust Post		15,936.00
	Roads and Bridges		12,500.00
	Electric Lines and Transformers		7,754.61
	Water Lines		21,516.00
	Electric Pumps		1,200.00
	Electric Motors		2,953.00
	Water Plant		15,000.00
	Coal		1,324.54
	Cattle Dipping Vat		750.00
	Miscellaneous Farm equipment and farm supplies as per revised list attached		49,265.27
79	Hogs		1,400.00
11	Feeder Cattle		1,250.00
21	Lambs		105.00
	Holstein Cattle		
82	Cows	10250.00	
21	Bred Heifers	1575.00	
40	Heifers and Yearlings	2000.00	
3	Bulls	1125.00	
19	Calves	380.00	
1	Steer	50.00	
166		15380.00	15,380.00
9	Mules		1,350.00
8	Horses @ $150.00	1200.00	
8	Horses @ $100.00	800.00	
		2000.00	2,000.00
			$841,934.42
	Hereford Cattle		
	Feed Inventories		

Revised appraisal.

November 18,1944

Mrs.Ethel V.Mars
930 Ashland Avenue
River Forest,Illinois.

My Dear Mrs.Mars:

I am enclosing herewith prepaid bill of lading on the things
that I shipped yesterday to you at Minocqua.I prepaid the
freight charges in the amount of $25.78.Included in the
shipment was the two grease guns,the power lawn mower,the
copper urn off the dining room table,the good Bendix washing
machine,bathroom scales and your chair.

Everything is going fine.Have not heard anything from Mr.Hoben
yet--don't suppose that they have priced it yet.The weather
has been nice here for the past few days but it is colder here
today but no rain yet.The van will be here Monday to get one
load of Mrs.Feeney's furniture and I am going to send what I
think they will need most first and I don't know when we will
be able to get the other van but hope real soon now.

I hope that you are feeling better.I suppose that you will be
going to Phoenix right away.

With kindest regards, Iam

                              Sincerely,

Conditions at the farm were changing rapidly. Articles were being moved and shipped daily. Some
items that had originally been thought to stay at the farm were now leaving.

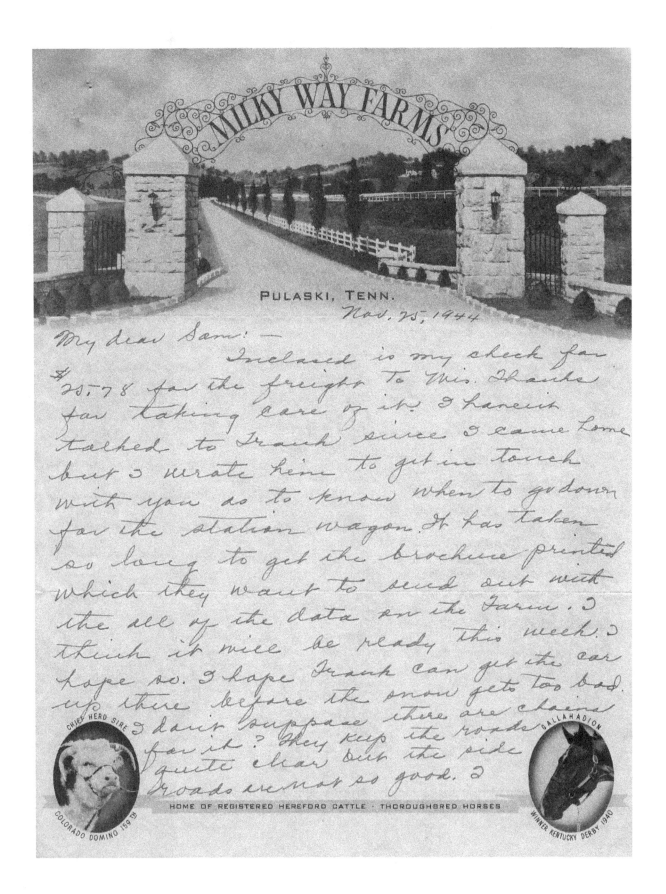

MILKY WAY FARMS

PULASKI, TENN.
Nov. 25, 1944

My dear Sam: —
Inclosed is my check for
$25.78 for the freight to Mrs. Thanks
for taking care of it. I haven't
talked to Frank since I came home
but I wrote him to get in touch
with you so to know when to go down
for the station wagon. It has taken
so long to get the brochure printed
which they want to send out with
the all of the data on the Farm. I
think it will be ready this week. I
hope so. I hope Frank can get the car
up there before the snow gets too bad.
I don't suppose there are chains
for it? They keep the roads
quite clear but the side
roads are not so good. I

CHIEF HERD SIRE
COLORADO DOMINO 159 TH

HOME OF REGISTERED HEREFORD CATTLE · THOROUGHBRED HORSES

GALLAHADION
WINNER KENTUCKY DERBY 1940

have been quite busy as Marie is still in Ariz. and I have to take care of the bills and urgent mail myself. I think she will be home by Mon or Tues. They called me this week and were "camping" in their new house & expecting the truck by Sat. today. I hope they got there OK. We are leaving on Monday Dec. 4th. on the Chief. Have been trying to do a little Xmas shopping as I will have so little time after I arrive in Phoenix. Have not been very well and have been having X Ray at the hospital which takes time. Tell Mrs. Fleming I have two down pillows I brought from Ariz. this spring & I want her to send them to me out there as I will need them. My address is the same Rt #7 Box 466 - Phoenix. Am writing Abe as he is so worried about where he is going to live. Am afraid the lumber people or who ever he is dealing with, are holding him up. Will you please look into it. Don't let them know I am helping him and see if he can get someone to build him a little house on Jennie Macs lot. You can call me if necessary.

Best Regards,

Adt V. Mars

It was unusual to receive a hand written letter from Mrs. Mars. This letter lets the reader know that her health was failing her and you get the feeling that she was worried. She also shows a real concern for

Abraham Macklin who she refers to as Abe. She was going to build him a house and was concerned that he did not have the knowledge to keep from getting beat by a contractor. She wanted Sam Collins to help him and see that he did not get cheated.

ETHEL V. MARS

930 ASHLAND AVENUE	MARLANDS	MILKY WAY FARMS
RIVER FOREST	MINOCQUA	PULASKI
ILLINOIS	WISCONSIN	TENNESSEE

Dec. 2, 1944

Dear Sam:

This won't be much of a letter. First place this typewritter is something left over from the "Chicago Fire" and then too - I am trying to get things lined up as Mrs. Mars is leaving for Phoenix this coming Monday. I just returned from there Thursday and won't go out again until aft er the 1st of the year.

Anyway - this is what I wanted to write you at this time --

Mrs. Mars wants to give some of the Help at the Farm Clubhouse a christmas gift of money and decided to ask you to do it for her as she does not know their last names - so I am enclosing her check made payable to you for $65.00 and will you please distribute it as follows:

```
        Zena Mae ----------- 10.00
        Melissa------------- 10.00
        Lizzie B------------ 10.00
        Lena---------------- 10.00
        Dorthula------------ 10.00
        Patrick ------------ 10.00
        Albert-------------- 5.00
```

Thanks very much Sam. Will write you again soon. Hope your family is well.

Best regards,

Marie

Mrs. Mars directed Marie Quinlan to have Sam Collins give these Christmas gifts to select clubhouse employees. The last two letters show the compassion Mrs. Mars had for her employees.

December 10,1944

Mrs.Ethel V.Mars
R#7 Box 466
Phoenix,Arizona

My Dear Mrs.Mars:

Pardon my delay in answering your letter but have been quite
busy and have just neglected writing you.

Everything is going along fine.We have been having some right
cold weather and quite a lot of rain.Had a little snow one day
last week but it didn't last very long--melted the same day that
it fell.

Regarding the Buick Station Wagon.We can send it anytime that you
think it should go.Of course,you know that Alan has to have something to drive when he is back here and I don't know just how
much driving back and forth to Nashville we will have to do in
bringing prospects to look at the farm.I can use the coupe that
I am driving if there are just two but if there is more we will
have to make some other arrangements.There has been no one here
to look yet but I should think that they will begin to go to
coming in,in the next few days.I can appreciate your wanting to
get it up to the Lake before the snow gets so bad and you just
write me what you think best to do and I will do it.I don't know
how much Alan will be here and he will need something to drive
    when he does come in for a few days.You can let me know
    what you think best to do.

Regarding the house for Abe.Looks like Abe has gotten confused
on the rules and regulations regarding building new homes at
this time.The first thing that a person has to do now is to get
a permit to build a house from the War Production Board which
takes some time and is very hard to get.He is filing an application
with them to get permission to build a house and I don't know
how long it will take to go through.Then the figuresthat he sent
you seem a little high but it looks like that is the best he can
do now under the existing circumstances.There is no one around
Pulaski that will contract a lock and key job as all of them
have quit contracting under the existing circumstances regarding
building new homes and the figures he sent you cover the material
and an estimate on the labor and the Lumber Dealer that made them
for him will not guarantee the labor to run what he estimates
because he is only figureing on the material and it will be up to
Abe to get the labor to build the house and of course that can
run more less than the estimate.It appears to me that the best
thing for Abe to do would be to wait until the situation got to
where a person could build a house without a permit and then
when that time comes these local lumber dealers will be back
contracting houses and we could figure with two or three of them
and get them to bidding on building the house instead of letting
them hold him up at this time on a house that probably would not
be nearly as good as a house he could get built a little later
when this situation eased up some and as I have said before there
is not a dealer here at this time that will take a lock and key
contract on a house and that will be the best way for him to get
a house built instead of buying the lumber from some person and
dealing with other people on building it--someone has to be over
the labor to see that they do a good job of building.I will let
 you know how he comes out on getting the permit as that is
    the first thing that has to be done and then if he gets
    the permit--I will let you know and then we can figure
    out some way maybe to get the house built as cheap as
    possible.However,permits are hard to get and I am
    doubting him being able to get one.

I got the check from Marie for Christmas gifts to the colored
girls and I will take care of that for you.I also want to
thank you for the nice Christmas gift.You don't know how very
much we did appreciate it.Again I want to thank you for same.

I still have not been able to get another truck to bring the
rest of the furniture for Mrs.Feeney.I hope that I got enough
of the things that they really needed in the first load.I have
been worrying the truck people to death but they just have not
had anything available so far that will take care of the
furniture that is left here.Maybe something will show up in
the next few days. Hope the first load got there in good shape.
                    To
I presume that we will go having lots of activity around here
now since they have priced the farm. Sure do hope they will be
able to make the sale and leave the home for me off as I surely
do want to own that home as I feel that I would rather live
there than any other place,as I have been here at the farm so
long that it feels like home and I hope that I can get that place
and keep it as long as I live. Mrs.Mars you don't know how very
much I do appreciate your helping me to get it and I will always
keep in memory of working for the grandest person in the world.

I surely do hope that you are feeling much better and that you
will soon be much improved.

With kindest personal regards,I am

                    Sincerely,

I hope that this three page letter didn't bore you. It gives you a real feeling what was going on in
December 1944 as Milky Way Farms is about to be sold and change the life of a great number of
devoted workers that have been loyal to Mrs. Mars. It is fairly obvious that Mrs. Mars' health is
deteriorating rapidly. Sam Collins is trying to help Abraham (Abe) with his house and advice to Mrs.
Mars about same. Sam Collins would like very much to have the house that we lived in taken out of the
sale so that he could buy it and continue to live there. This was our home and my parents loved it.

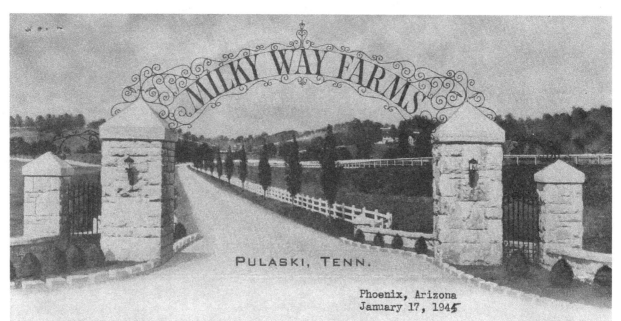

PULASKI, TENN.

Phoenix, Arizona
January 17, 1945

Mr. Sam Collins, Jr.
Milky Way Farms
Pulaski, Tenn.

Dear Sam:

I talked to Mr. Hoben and, while we have not had the bonuses confirmed by the Government, he suggested that we advance the money to the three men, Pete Graves, Ed McNeese and Henry Davis, and ask them to sign notes. Later, when we receive the okeh from the Government, we will issue new checks and they can take up their notes. This seems to be the only way we can handle the matter at the present time. We have to be very careful how these things are handled, as you know there are penalties attached to any deviation from the laws laid down by the O.P.A. and any other governmental department. I presume that Mr. Hurley has gotten in touch with you.

I have suggested to the Company that the balance of the cattle, which Alan and Patty are taking, be shipped before very long on account of weather conditions out here. Alan feels that he can handle them with the men he now has, so it will not be necessary to take Frank Thurman away until the Farm is sold. As Alan and Patty are in Denver this week I have not told him anything about this suggestion, although we had talked it over previously. As soon as I know definitely I will let you know in order to arrange for cars.

I am feeling pretty well and the weather is delightful.

Wishing you a Happy and Prosperous New Year and with kindest personal regards to all, I am

Sincerely,

Ethel V. Mars

ETHEL V. MARS

HOME OF REGISTERED HEREFORD CATTLE · THOROUGHBRED HORSES

EVM:Q

This letter gives you an insight into what was taking place with the best cattle on the farm.

Mr.Pete Graves
Milky Way Hereford Ranch
R#7 Box 424
Phoenix,Arizona

Dear Pete:

I am enclosing herewith statement of your earnings for 1945
as sent me by Mr.Hurley of Mars Inc.,to be forwarded to you.
This is the amount that they reported as being paid you in
1945 by them.

You really cleaned up at Denver.I am surely glad that you did
clean the boys.You will be tough from now on,as long as old
Larry is doing the job that he has been doing.Guess that you
will be in Phoenix for a while.Guess the weather is plenty
chilly in Springerville now.I imagine that you had some nice
visits with Brownie at Denver.He hasn't gotten home yet.

No need of me trying to tell you all the news around here,since
you have seen Brownie.I imagine that he has given it all to you.
Write and give me the lowdown on things out there.There are
some bad stories going around in the newspapers about the boss
and the Mrs.--what is really happening and what is going to happen
to things out there--Pete,I have heard so many rumors would
appreciate it if you would write me the correct dope on things and
what is going to happen.I will hold it in strict confidence.
Best regards to you and your family.

                              Sincerely,

This letter is unique in that it gives the reader an insight into what was going on around the sale of the farm, the movement of items including the best cattle to Arizona. The rumors that Sam Collins is referring to are about the marriage of Alan and Patty. Pete Graves had already moved to Arizona with Alan Feeney at the Milky Way Hereford Ranch in Phoenix, Arizona. Sam wanted to know if the rumors of their impending divorce were true or not.

In keeping with my plan to try and keep this in chronological order I am going to put the inventory of the clubhouse here. If you were a prospective buyer you would want to know what you were going to get for your investment. So bear with me because this is a part of the history of the farm.

Inventory Club House Milky Way Farms as of March 1,1948

Room No

1--Left Wing Down Stairs	No. Of Articles	Name Of Articles
	2	Leather Chair (2)
	1	Lamp Table
	1	Lamp
	1	Desk
	1	Straight Chair
	1	Smoking Chair
	1	Book Case
	1 Picture	
	1	Vase
	1	Liquer Cabinet
		Floor Carpeted

2		
	1 Pr	Drapes
	1	Chaise
	1	Chest Draw ers
	2	Single Beds
	1	Bedside Table
	1	Chair
	1	Lamp
		Floor Carpeted

3		
	1 Pr.	Drapes
	1	Irioning Table
	1	Ironing Board
	1	Book Shelf
	1	Clothe Dryer

4		
	1 Pr.	Drapes
	1	Double Bed
	1	Chest Drawers
	1	Mirror
	1	Leather Topped Taboret
	1	Floor Lamp
	1	Chair
	1	Bedside Table
		Floor Carpeted

5		
	1	Breakfast Table
	2	Benches
	1	Vase
	1	Oriental Rug
	1	Trophy Cabinet
	3	Potted Plants
		Drapes
		Linoleum

Inventory Club House Milky Way Farms as of March 1, 1945

Left Corridor Down Stairs

4	Chairs
1	Jacobean Press
1	Ten Foot Console Antique
1	Tall Copper Lamp
1	Utility Seat
1	Oriental Throw Rug
1	Large Book Shelf
1	Chest Drawers
	Corridor Carpeted

Lobby

1	Chair
1	Mirror
1	Black Leather Couch
1	Red Leather Chair
1	Black Leather Chair
1	Console (With Drawers)
2	Pottery Wine Jug Lamps
1	Potted Plant
	Red Drapes
	Lobby Carpeted

Living Room

2	Eight Foot Couches
6	Leather Chairs
4	Leather Covered Stools
2	Tall Back Chairs
1	Antique Refractory Table
6	Potted Palms
1	Standard Fern
1	Steinway Grand Piano
1	Piano Stool
1	Radio
1	Oriental Screen
1	Bookcase and Cabinet
3	Floor Lamps
6	Standard Copper Lamps
2	Brass Mantle Lamps
1	Large Horse Painting
	Red Drapes
	Living Room Carpeted
4	Tapestry Pillows
1	Brass Smoking Stand
2	Table Lamps
1	Large Fire Screen
1 Pr	Andirons
1	Large Vase
	Fireplace Fixtures
2	Couch Tables
1	Small Oriental Rug
	Carpeted

Inventory Club House Milky Way Farms as of March 1,1945

Right Wing Corridor

3	Chairs
1	Mirror
1	Large Book Cabinet
2	Antique Desks
1	Antique Chest
1	Copper Antique Chest
1	Small Oriental Rug
	Carpeted

Room No. 1--Right Wing Down Stairs

2	Single Beds (Twin)
2	Bedside Tables
2	Lamps
1	Chest
1	Mirror
2	Wing Chairs
2	Prints
	Drapes
2	White Velvet Spreads

Room No. 2--Right Wing Down Stairs

	Venetian Blinds
2	16th Century Canopy Beds
1	Chest
1	Mirror
1	Vase
1	Table
3	Lamps
1	Chair
	Carpeted and Drapes
2	Bedspreads
1	Dressing Table and Seat

Room No. 3--Right Wing Down Stairs

1	Double Hollywood Bed
1	Chest Drawers
2	Oriental Lamps
2	Bedside Tables
1	Round Table
2	Lamps
	Brass Firewood Fixtures
	Carpeted
	Drapes and Venetian Blinds
2	Chairs
1	Mirror
	Chintz Quilted Bed Spreads
2	Accasional Seats

Room No. 4 Right Wing

	Curtains
1	Couch
2	End Tables
2	Lamps
1	Picture
2	Chairs
1	Seat
1	Chest
1	Coffee Table

Inventory Club House Milky Way Farms as of March 1,1945

Lower Right Wing Sun Porch
        Down Stairs

	3	Chairs
	1	Wicker Chaise Chair
	1	Table
Dining Room	1	Banquet Table
	22	Chairs
	1	Extension Dining Table
	1	Serving Table
	1	Large Buffett
	1	Small Buffett
	1	Marble Top Table
	2	Standard Iron Lamps
	20	Potted Plants
	1	Large Painting (Bull)
	2	Brass Mantel Lamps
	1	Iron Fire Seat
n		Screen and Iron Fixture Holder
Butler's Pantry	2	Frigidaires
	1	Utility Cabinet
	1	Large Toaster
	1	Large Electric Mixer
Kitchen	1	Electric Orange Reamer
	1	Plain Orange Reamer
	5	Skillets
	5	Pans
	2	Baking Pans
	5	Muffing Rings
	3	Granite Percualtors
	15	Pots and Pans (Granite)
	3	Milk Pitchers
	3	Aluminum Trays
	1	Potato Ricer
	1	Coffee Strainer
	1	Vegetable Grater
	1	Butcher Knife
	3	Cooking Spoons
	2	Spatulas
	1	Vegetable Chopper
	8	Odd Spoons and Knives
	1	Potato Peeler
	1	Can Opener
	1	Four Over Gas Stove
	1	Monel Topped Table
	1	Enamel Topped Table
	1	Charcoal Aluminim Broiler
	1	Hotel Size Range
	6	Kitchen Chairs

Inventory Club House Milky Way Farms as of March 1, 1945

Sun Porch Up Stairs
        Right Wing

1	Desk
2	Chair
1	Couch
2	Lamps
2	End Tables

Right Wing Up Stairs
Room No. 1

1	Triple Bed
1	Chest
1	Stool
2	Chairs
1	Table
1	Telephone
1	Lamp

Room No. 2

1	Twin Bed
1	Table
1	Lamp
1	Dresser
1	Mirror
1	Chair
	Carpeted

Room No. 3

1	Single Bed
1	Small Cabinet
1	Table
1	Lamp
1	Chair
1	Dressing Table
	Inlaid Linoleum Rug

Room No. 4

2	Beds (Twin)
2	Chests
2	Chairs
1	Table
1	Lamp
1	Ptterman

Upper Tight Wing Hallway

	Carpeted
1	Large Chest
1	Antique Desk
1	Drop Leaf Table
2	Chairs
1	Lamp

Right Wing Attic

1	Artificial Fire Place
1	Wicker Stool
1	Smoking Stand
1	Three Tiered Table
4	Perch Wire Screens
6	Billiard Table Chairs
12	Straight Odd Chairs
9	Bed Steds
2	Chest Drawers
1	Roll Discarded Linoleum
1	Sunshine Carbon Lamp
7	Pictures
6	Mirrors

Inventory Club House Milky Way Farms as of March 1,1948

Cedar Linen Room
Upper Right Wing Attic

1	Cloths Hamper
1	Bed Pan
12	Tennis Balls
3	Curtain Rods
12	Cue Sticks (Billiard)
1	Chair

Basement

1	Billiard Table
3	Curtain Rods
1	Leather Chair
1	Iron Bound Chest

Laundry Room

2	Large Ironing Tables
1	Ironing Board
1	Chair
1	Ironing Stool
1,	Large Mangle

Basement(Side)

1	Broom Holder
1	Roller Coaster Rack
2	Children Carpentering Table
1	Small Table
4	Used Doors (Stored)

Upper Left Wing
Room No. 1

2	Beds (Twin)
	Damask Spreads
1	Table
1	Lamp
1	Chest Drawers
1	Mirror
	Carpets and Drapes
1	Chair

Room No. 2

1	Double Bed
	Satan Spreads
	Carpeting and Drapes
2	Bedside Tables
1	Chest
1	Mirror
2	Chairs
1	Lamp

Room No. 3

1	Dpuble Bed
	Satan Spreads
	Carpeted and Drapes
1	Chest
1	Bedside Table
1	Lamp
1	Chair
1	Mirror

Upper Left Wing
Room No. 4

	Carpeted
	Drapes
2	Beds (Twin)
	Velvet Bed Spreads
1	Bedside Table
1	Chair
1	Chest Drawers
1	Mirror
1	Lamp

Room No. 5

2	Beds (Twins)
	Damask Spreads
1	Chair
1	Bedside Table
1	Chest
1	Mirror
	Carpeted and Drapes

Room No. 6

1	Double Bed
1	Chest Drawers
1	Mirror
1	Table
1	Lamp
1	Leather Top Bench
1	Chair
2	Prints
	Carpeted and Drapes

Two Nursery Rooms Unfurnished

Left Wing Upper Corridor

1	Red Leather Couch
2	Red Leather Chairs
1	Tall Chair (Antique)
6	Straight Chairs
1	Picture
	Carpeted

Cedar Room in Left Wing Attic

45	Winter Wool Blankets Satin Bound for single and double beds
45	White Summer Blankets single and Double
2	Sets Linen Damask Covers for Banquet Table
6	Counterpanes

Inventory Club House Milky Way Farm as of March 1,1945

Storage In Attic	4	Rolls Discarded Carpeting
	1	Roll Rubber Carpeting Padding
	3	Tin Boxes
	2	Venetian Blinds
	1	Porch Couch
	4	Tables
	2	Porch
	10	Dining Room Chairs
		Legs and sections for dining Tabb
	1	Iron Bed
	1	Wooden Bed
	1	Chest Drawers
	1	Mirror
	1	Small Cabinet
	1	High Chair
	2	Stools
	4	House Chairs
	2	Small Tables
		Billiard Table Accessories
	1	Kitchen Chair
	1	Invalid Table
	1	Chair Cushion
	1	Coffee Urn
	2	Bird Cages
	2	Bundles Ozite
	1	Double Electric Waffle Iron
Linen Closet (Cedar)	1	Card Table
	1	Chair
	80	Luncheon Doilies
	40	Small Napkins
	60	Large Napkins
	6	Linen Table Cloths
	26	Napkins
	80	Double and Single Irish LinenSheets
	51	Double-Single Percale Sheets
	18	Winter Green Blankets
	15	White Summer Blankets
	20	Bed Pads
	22	Linen Hand Towels
	14	Cotton Woven Bedspreads
	2	Tufted Spreads
	22	Doilies and Dresser Throws
	42	Pillow Cases
	74	Bath Towels
	52	Wash Cloths
	25	Bath Rugs
	10	Rag Rugs
	24	Triple Size Sheets
	2	Triple Size Blankets
	8	Triple Size Spreads
	31	Pillows
Broom Closet	2	Hoover Cleaners
	1	Bissell Sweeper
	1	Utility Shelf
	1	Chair

Inventory Club House Milky Way Farms as of March 1, 1945

Silver	30 Knives
	16 Soup Spoons
	17 Dinner Forks
	17 Demitasse Spoons
	25 Teaspoons
	21 Dessert and Table Spoons
	20 Salad Forks
	4 Gravey Ladels
	14 Butter Knives
	52 Cocktail Forks
	3 Carving Sets
	1 Ice Tings
	2 Sugar Tongs
Black Knight China	82 Dinner Plates
	71 Salad Plates
	40 Breakfast Plates
	31 Demitasse Cups
	56 Saucers
	42 Coffee Cups
	24 Large Dessert Crystal Plates
	46 Small Dessert Crystal Plates
	4 Pickles Dishes
	38 Ice Compotes
	12 Bouillion
	26 Glasses
	5 Jelly Dishes
	12 Sherbert Dishes
	3 Silver Gravey Bowls
	3 Silver Cream Pitchers
	3 Silver Sugar Bowls
	10 Silver Platters
	11 Odd Silver Bowls
	2 Silver Canoy Platters
	2 Silver Serving Bowls
	7 Pyrex Dishes
	3 Silver Coffee Servers
	15 Silver Goblets
	14 Salt and Pepper Shakers
	8 Silver Water Pitchers
	6 Silver Ash Trays

The inventory of the Milky Way Farms clubhouse as of March 1, 1945

I am going to risk wearing the reader out with descriptions of the farm and those things that a prospective buyer would like to know. The next six pages will be the prospectus that a serious person would want to have to get a synopsis of the farm.

Barn---270' x 36' Suitable for Sheep or Cattle
Sheep Dipping Vat near barn.

Steer Feeding Barn---414' x 80'---Suitable for feeding around 1000 head steers.
Water Troughs in barn and feed lots. Four feed lots and barn cut into four
feeding sections. Set of stock scales in pen where cattle can be weighed while
on feed at any desired weighing period. Barn equipped with a conveyor to be
used in putting baled hay in loft. Enough loft space to store approximately
400 tons of hay and feed racks built where hay can be put in racks from loft of
barn. Also sufficient grain troughs in barn and self feeders in feed lots.
Barn equipped with lights.

Slaughter House---Suitable for slaughtering steers-hogs and lamb s. Equipped
with chain hoist for hanging carcass.

Corn Crib---Suitable for storing ear corn---holds approximately 12 ,500 barrels
of ear corn or 62,500 bushels of ear corn. Equipped with electric hoist for
unloading trucks and wagons and corn is moved into crib from unloading chute by
a conveyor and is placed in any section of the crib desired by a conveyor. When
corn is ready to be removed from crib can be pushed out of crib whose floor is
built on an angle by hand into a conveyor on side of crib and corn is carried on
the conveyor into the sheller. Equipped with power and necessary motors to
operate all conveyor equipment.

Feed Mill---Corn goes by conveyor into #10 John Deere corn sheller and after corn
is shelled pours direct from sheller into a storage bin that holds approximately
4000 bushels of shelled corn and the cobs are run thru a Jacobsen Hammer Mill
and ground, and fall into a cob bin and the shucks are blown a short distance
away thru a pipe and fall directly into a shuck baler and can be baled and have
to be baled as you shell the corn. Mill also equipped with storage bins for
Cotton Seed Meal-Sweet Feed Supplement such as Tarkio or Steer Fatena and also
bin for cracked corn. Sufficient motors to run all feed mill equipment and then
the corn can be taken out of storage bins by gravity and goes directly into a
#30 Blue Streak Hammer Mill and is cracked or ground and blown into a storage
bin where it can be taken out as cracked corn thru a Sprout Waldron feed mixing
conveyor or can be mixed with cotton seed meal and any kind of supplement into
any proportions desired and after being mixed run into a wagon or truck where it
can be fed in the feed lots or any barns where it is desired to be hauled. Also
cob bin equipped with conveyor for taking cobs out of bin and loading into truck
or wagon. Mill equipped with all motors necessary to operate. Mill made of
concrete.

Stone barn---Suitable for feeding and running cattle and cows and calves---Has calf
creeps in barn---hay racks in barn for cows and also hay racks outside barn for
feeding hay.

Wooden Barn---330' x 60' Suitable for cattle---Equipped with 33 tie stalls---30 stalls
for turning cattle loose and one fourth of barn fixed to run a bunch of cattle
loose. Loft space that will hold approximately 375 tons of hay and equipped
with conveyor to be used in putting baled hay into loft---Necessary stocks-chutes
and lots for handling cattle. Barn equipped with lights and water.

Stone Barn---Hereford show cattle barn---equipped with 54 stalls for cattle with
automatic water fountains---Has a sales pavilion, feed room and wash room. Lights
and hot water heater.

Wooden Barn---487' x 45'. Suitable for horses---Equipped with 54 horse stalls---
wash room and feed room and exercise ring all the way around the inside of the
barn. Water and lights.

SINCE MILKY WAY FARMS IS IN ACTUAL OPERATION, THE ABOVE IS AN APPROXIMATE INVENTORY
AND IS NOT GUARANTEED TO BE AN ACCURATE INVENTORY.

Wooden Garage Building---Large enough to house trucks and equipment. Has a parts room---Mechanic work room---Carpenter Shop equipped with woodworking machine and planer and other carpenter equipment---Storage space for lumber---All kinds of garage equipment such as air compressor--battery charger---electric and aceytelene welding outfits--hoist for lifting trucks and auto's and hydraulic lift, etc. A good garage and carpenter shop building. Water and lights. 290' x 75'.

Wooden Hay Storage Barn--Will store approximately 750 tons of hay.

Wooden barn---Suitable for storing tools and can be used to feed some cattle in winter if necessary.

Wooden Dairy Barn---Equipped with 56 stanchions for milking cows concrete feed troughs and concrete floor--3 unit DeLaval Magnetic milker---Electric water heater---Can racks---Electric Melotte Cream Separator---one 14 can Wilson Milk Cooler Box--one 7 can milk cooler box---one aerator for cooling milk---5 stalls for use in calving time---one feed room---Vats to wash milking equipment---Lights and water.

Wooden Blacksmith Shop--Equipped with forge---All necessary blacksmith tools--- Lathe and drills and grinding equipment---also used as storage place for paint and tools and farms supplies.

Wooden Barn---Suitable for Horses or Mules--18 stalls and feed room. Water and lights.

Wooden Horse barn---8 tie stalls and 4 box stalls---equipped with light and water---Feed Room.

Wooden Oat Storage House--Will hold approximately 5000 bu. oats---feed by gravity into Barrentine Oat Roller with capacity of 90 bushels per hour and necessary storage space for storing rolled oats.

Wooden Horse Barns--8 stalls-feed room and wash room---one quarter mile track nearby. Water and Lights.

Stone Tack Rooms--Sufficient space for office--all tack equipment --warming room and blacksmith room. Water and Lights.

Stone Barn---300' x 50'. Suitable for cattle or storing hay. Racks and feed troughs in barn.

Stone Barn--210' x 60'--Suitable for cattle or storing hay. Racks and feed troughs in barn. Chute and lot for handling cattle.

Stone Barn---300' x 50'--Suitable for cattle or storing hay. Racks and feed troughs in barn.

Stone Barn--408' x 35'--Suitable for cattle or sheep. Racks and feed troughs in barn--Also some stalls.

Stone Barn--260' x 60'--Sales cattle barn--28 tie stalls-15 stalls for running loose--1 wash room--1 feed room--1 supply room---water and lights in barn-- suitable chutes and lots for cattle handling.

Stone Barn--260' x 75'--Thoroughbred Horse barn--24 horsestalls--Tack Room-- Feed Room--Wash Room--office--lights and water--5/8 mile track nearby. Walking ring inside barn around stalls for cooling out horses.

SINCE MILKY WAY FARMS IS IN ACTUAL OPERATION, THE ABOVE IS AN APPROXIMATE INVENTORY AND IS NOT GUARANTEED TO BE AN ACCURATE INVENTORY.

BUILDINGS

CLUB HOUSE-----Stone Building with tile roof--

                Entrance-Lobby with wash room
                Living Room with large fireplace
                Tile Floor front porch
                Dining Room with water fountain and fireplace
                Recreation Room Downstairs
                Butlers Pantry
                Kitchen
                Laundry Room Downstairs
                Meat Storage Room downstairs sufficient for large family, an d storage space
                for vegetables in cold storage room.
                Back porch at kitchen
                Lower Right Wing---Master bedroom-bath-sitting room and entrance on sun porch.
                                Master guest room-bath-entrance on sun porch.
                                Guest room-bath
                                Large long corridor
                Lower Left Wing----Linen Room(Cedar)
                                Wash Room
                                Cloak Room
                                4 Bed Rooms---with 2 shower baths
                                Small Dining or Storage Room
                Right Upper Wing--master bedroom-dressing room-bath
                                1 Nursery room connected, or bedroom
                                1 large 4 bed childrens dormatory room or bedroom
                                1 Childs room or bedroom-connecting bath or shower
                                Picture window sitting room
                                Large Hall
                                Large attic
                Left Upper Wing----8 Bedrooms
                                4 showers
                                Large Attic
                                Cedar Linen Room
                                Large Corridor

                From 1 to 3 closets in all rooms. Hall closets in all corridors Soft
                water in Master rooms. Steam heat piped from central heating plant. Wood
                or coal range in kitchen. Pyrofax gas stove in kitchen.

SERVANTS COTTAGE:
                Living room with fire place
                1-four bed room
                2 bedrooms
                2 baths
                Large kitchen and dining room--can be used for bedroom
                Built in cupboards
                Large porch
                Steam heat

SWIMMING POOL AND TENNIS COURT:
                Asphalt Tennis Court with wire enclosure
                Swimming pool will hold approximately 60,000 gallons of water and is a
                tile pool with 2 sets of diving boards. Equipped with Permutit filters .
                Water is turned constantly and is chlorinated with chlorine and is up to
                date in every respect as to sanitation.

                Office Building

SINCE MILKY WAY FARMS IS IN ACTUAL OPERATION, THE ABOVE IS AN APPROXIMATE INVENTORY AND
IS NOT GUARANTEED TO BE AN ACCURATE INVENTORY.

Trench Silo with a capacity of approximately 1050 tons---Concrete Bottom.

Cattle Dipping Vat sufficient for dipping cattle and one of the best types.

Rock Crusher that will crush all rock needed for roads on farm and for any concrete work that might have to be done.

Ice plant that will freeze one ton of ice every 24 hours in addition to furnishing refrigeration for meat storage room at Club House and used to cool water at Club House and office---Plant in good condition.

Water System that furnishes water for most of farm houses and most all the barns and Club House and swimming Pool---Reservoir has a capacity of 126,860 gallons and water comes from a cave spring and is treated with Chlorine as it comes from the spring with a Wallace and Tiernan Chlorinator and we put about 5 parts per million of chlorine and the water is then pumped in the reservoir and is chlorinated while in the reservoir. As the water comes out of the reservoir the chlorine is filtered out by a Universal Water Filter system and we have as pure a type of water as is possible to make and it is fed by gravity to all the buildings that it serves.

Have another reservoir that is located above feeder barn and water can be pumped from creek or spring but the water is good for livestock only and this reservoir has a capacity of 141,750 gallons and was used by us in our steer feeding operations and the water from this reservoir flows by gravity to all the barns that it serves.

Have 29 barns on the farm including slaughter house and corn crib.

Have 48 Houses and Cottages on the farm.

Have 105 acres of Alfalfa hay at this time and are in the process of sowing another 80 acres at this time---making a total acreage of Alfalfa for next year of 185 acres. Cut the hay from four to five times per year and will make an average of over 3 tons per acre an average year.

Have over 55 miles of plank fence---all painted white.

Have nearly twenty miles of road on the farm leading to all parts of the farm.

Farm is well watered by springs and creek.

Pastures are arranged and fenced suitable for carrying on a large purebred cattle breeding operation---well arranged for both pasture breeding and hand breeding of animals.

SINCE MILKY WAY FARMS IS IN ACTUAL OPERATION, THE ABOVE IS AN APPROXIMATE INVENTORY AND IS NOT GUARANTEED TO BE AN ACCURATE INVENTORY.

<u>EQUIPMENT AND SUPPLIES</u>

10	Two Horse Farm Wagons
220	Gallons Milky Way Green Paint
1525	Gallons Milky Way White Fence Paint
55	Gallons Milky Way White Concrete Paint
	Blacksmith Tools and Shop Equipment
2	International Dump Hay Rakes
1	One Horse Wagon
1	Cut Off Wood Saw for use with Tractor
1	One Horse Disc
1	Horse Drawn Roller
2	Tractor Drawn Lime Spreaders
2	International Power Manure Spreaders
1	Tractor Drawn Cultipacker
1	Horse Drawn Manure Spreader
1	Road Grader
1	Concrete Mixer
1	International Horse Drawn Side Delivery Hay Rake
1	International Tractor Drawn Side Delivery Hay Rake
1	Gas Shovel Ensley ½ Yards with clam shell and dipper
1	Lime Mill
1	Heavy Duty Rock Wagon
1	John Deere 3 Disc Tractor Plow
1	John Deere 3 Gang 16" #66 Tractor plow on rubber
1	Heavy Duty John Deere Sub Soiler
1	John Deere Double Disc 16" Disc
1	D4 Caterpillar Diesel Tractor
1	1937 Diamond T Trailer Truck
1	1937 Diamond T 1½ Ton Stake Body Truck
2	1937 Diamond T Dump Trucks
1	1941 Diamond T Pickup Truck
1	1942 Ford Station Wagon
1	1931 Sterling Water Wagon
1	1935 Ford Coupe
1	1934 Plymouth Coupe
2	Baughman Lime Spreaders that work on dump trucks
1	John Deere Van Brunt Drill 14ft.
1	Case Pickup Hay Baler
	Stock Baling Wire
1	Ann Arbor Hay Baler with pickup and Automatic Threader
1	Fox Pickup Cutter with pickup and mower bar attachment
1	Marvel Seed and Fertilizer Distributor
2	Air Compressors---1 Buhl and 1 Ingersoll Rand
1	Farm All A Tractor on Rubber
1	Allis Chalmers B Model Tractor on Rubber
1	Minneapolis-Moline RTU Tractor and Feed Wagon on Rubber
1	International T 20 Trac Tractor
1	International Tractor Mower 7 Ft. Blade
2	John Deere Tractor Mowers 7 Ft. Blades
2	John Deere Big 4 Horse Drawn Mowers on Rubber
2	Massey Harris Horse Drawn Mowers on Steel
	Jack Hammers, Hose, Battery and Quarry Equipment
1	Ottawa Wood Saw and tree faller attachment for tractor
1	Wilco Electric Welder at Garage
1	Linde Aire Acytelene Welder-guages-cylinder-rack-tips and cutting torch
	Miscellaneous Garage tools and equipment not owned by mechanic
	Stock of repairs for Auto's-truck-tractors-mowers and other farm equipment
1	Parkes #117 Planer 20" Endurance Planer
1	Parkes #187 Model A Woodworking Machine Planing mill special
	Miscellaneous carpenters tools and equipment not owned by carpenters
	Stock of lumber for all kinds of miscellaneous repairs and fencing lumber
300	Sqs. Barrett 210# Roofing
23	Sqs. Barrett Giant Individual Shingles
2785	Gals. Barrett Elastigum Roof Coating
	Miscellaneous Plumber equipment and supplies
	Miscellaneous Electric equipment and supplies
	Miscellaneous Saddle Horse Equipment
	Miscellaneous Race Horse Equipment
	Miscellaneous Mule Equipment and Harness
	Miscellaneous Farm Equipment and supplies too small to list
	Office equipment, Desks, Safe, Filing Cabinets, Typewriters, Adding machines and Monroe Calculator, etc.
	Veterinary Supplies and equipment

SINCE MILKY WAY FARMS IS IN ACTUAL OPERATION, THE ABOVE IS AN APPROXIMATE INVENTORY AND IS NOT GUARANTEED TO BE AN ACCURATE INVENTORY.

```
500   Bags Cement
      Milk Room equipment-1-14 can Wilson Cooler-1-7 Can Esco cooler-1 Areator
      1 Melotte Electric Cream Separator-1 Electric water Heater-2 Sets scales
      Heaters-cook stoves and hot water tanks in tenant houses
  3   Electric conveyors for baled hay or sacked feed
      1-20 ft. long and 2-30 ft. long with electric motors
  1   Hoist for lifting barrels and rocks
      Stock Dynamite and Caps and electric exploders
      Rock Crusher
  2   Sets Fairbanks-Morse 20 Ton Capacity Scales
  8   Electric Water Pumps Various Sizes
      Approximately 35 Electric Motors ¼ HP to 50 HP
      Miscellaneous Farm Equipment and Supplies
      Approximately 250 Tons Coal
```

Approximately 5 1/2 miles electric lines including approximately 35 transformers of various sizes from 5 KW to 25 KW.

```
Approximately 2 1/2 miles 4" Water Line
      "       1 1/2  "   2"    "      "
      "       1 1/2  "   2½"   "      "
      "       2      "   1"    "      "
```

SINCE MILKY WAY FARMS IS IN ACTUAL OPERATION, THE ABOVE IS AN APPROXIMATE INVENTORY AND IS NOT GUARANTEED TO BE AN ACCURATE INVENTORY.

The last six pages have been that prospectus that you would have gotten if you were truly interested.

In early December, 1944 H. H. Hoben, the Assistant General Manager of Mars Inc. in Chicago made the announcement that Milky Way Farms was being offered for sale. Rumor of this had been circulating for a few months before this official announcement. In his announcement he stated that Milky Way Farms is a complete operational organization. It includes show barns, breeding barns, blacksmith shops, ice plant, miles of paved roads, water system, complete equipment, ample tenant houses, swimming pool and a magnificent clubhouse. He further stated that since Mr. Mars dream of making a significant contribution to the pure bred development in this country had been realized that he felt free to sell the farm provided that a purchaser willing to carry on this great work could be found. Two things that he did not mention that came into play in this decision was World War II which took a toll on everyone and Mrs. Mars' failing health. When the plans to sell the farm became known prominent members of the community tried to come up with ideas of how to keep the farm operating and a vital part of Giles County. One plan would have Giles County's representatives in the national legislature approach the federal government about purchasing the farm and use the site for a convalescent or general veteran's hospital. A committee comprised of Dr. W.J. Johnson, Hutton Brown, David Rhea, Erskine Sharp and G.B. Abernathy was formed to pursue the proper channels in Washington.

VOL. 2, NO. 4, APRIL, 1945 MARS, INC. 7 STAR EDITION

WE ARE "AT HIS SIDE"

BILL BOLDT HANGS UP BATTLE RECORD AT BASTOGNE

Word comes to us of Bill Boldt's experiences in besieged Bastogne via the Battalion news bulletin and a special letter of commendation to all members of the 705th Tank Destroyer's Battalion of which Bill is one of the tank commanders.

Among the first to reach the Siegfried line in the Moselle crossing, already commended for action at Plougestal, St. Malo, Brest and for the Brittany campaign, and besieged by the Germans at Bastogne, the battalion cost the enemy almost seven tanks for every gun he destroyed of theirs.

All of his friends are justly proud of Bill and his fellow fighters in their display of courage in the face of tremendous odds against them. Their stand and fight ultimately resulted in a definite reversal for the Nazis and put us again on the march. Bill has been awarded the Purple Heart for wounds received in battle.

Sam Lockwood contributes to the Red Cross drive. Minnie Jacobs waits her turn as volunteer workers Mrs. Jo Megall, Mrs. Genevieve Weren and Mrs. Myrtle Parrott efficiently handle employee subscriptions.

THEY ALSO SERVE—

Meet Martha Steingraber—C shift. The war is very near to Martha. Her work is important to her and so are the women who work with her on C shift. They help her forget. They comfort her when she can't forget. She has seven sons. Le Roy, 21, is a prisoner in Germany. A flight engineer and gunner of a B-24, he has won the air medal, flying cross and oak leaf cluster. Fred, 23, is a radio operator and gunner in Italy. Wilber, 18, has been sent overseas—destination—unknown. Her son-in-law, Ray Hosimer, is with the Seabees in the Philippines. Ray's two sisters, Florence and Mildred are Mars employees. Mildred has been with us since 1932 and Florence joined her in 1940. Martha's son, Allen, just 16 also joined Mars recently for after school hours. Martha Steingraber recently received word that her nephew, Ensign Parker, a navy fighter pilot in the South Pacific, was killed in action.

Buy Bonds—

(PICTURE AT LEFT)

Tena Anderson—A shift—has contributed 1000 hours to the Red Cross, rolling bandages, sewing and knitting sweaters and caps. She started Red Cross work before Pearl Harbor in Roselle, Illinois. A gold star mother—she has two sons serving the war—Chester, a radio operator in Italy and Ray, a mechanical engineer in a war plant in Arizona.

Hospital work is an important phase of Red Cross coverage. Loretta Degnan, Olive Healy and Mary Margaret Malahy give many hours each week to this activity. Already tired after a full day at the office they carry trays and assist with every function of hospital care.

Red Cross can't handle fund raising campaigns without workers to help in thousands of details and Lorraine Smith and Claire Sedore work nights after their duties at Mars are thru to assure the success of the Red Cross. When you work all day it takes real spunk to give your leisure time at night to more work.

EMPLOYEES AID RED CROSS DRIVE FOR FUNDS

Quietly attentive the various groups of diners in the Mars Cafeteria listened to Mrs. Baldwin Newman of Highland Park, representing the Chicago Chapter, appeal for 1945 Red Cross War Fund subscriptions. She reminded us that a worried soldier does not make a good soldier. The Red Cross relieves these worries so far as it is humanly possible.

There were many in her audience who were familiar with the work the Red Cross is doing. A gold star mother concentrated on her fork to keep the tears back when Mrs. Newman spoke of the wounded being cheered and aided by Red Cross workers. To another, a Red Cross nurse had written of her son's death. A young girl, pale from worry and grief over the report of her husband missing in action for 15 months, clenched her fists in her lap. She prays day and night that her husband may be in a prison camp, perhaps in Germany where she heard Mrs. Newman say packages containing medical supplies and high caloric foods were being received.

A guard, himself a Purple Heart veteran of the First World War, bowed his head in remembrance of his son, posthumously awarded the Purple Heart in World War Two, as she related the need for blood donors to save the lives of the fighters. A Grey Lady who attends a hospital two nights a week after a crowded working day respectfully gave her full attention.

The employees, anxious to participate, were assisted in filling out pledge cards by four attendant Red Cross workers who live in the vicinity and generously gave their time to our efforts to assure a successful Red Cross campaign for funds.

Malvina Donner who contributed to the Red Cross Blood Bank five times, shows nurse, Blanche LaMantia her bronze and silver pins awarded after the first three contributions.

The Milky Way News published by Mars Inc. highlighted its support for the troops and the war.

Giles County desperately wanted to keep Milky Way Farms on top and operational. However, their collective efforts failed and in May of 1945 Albert Noe Jr. purchased the farm for $575,000. The farm had been originally offered as a whole for $3,000,000, then reduced to $975,000. My father had shown the farm to many prospective buyers including Roy Rogers and Gene Autry but had no takers at that price. An agent representing Albert Noe approached my father and told him that Mr. Noe would offer a solid $575,000 for the entire operation. The leadership at Mars Inc. told him to close the deal. My father was asked by Mr. Noe to stay on as farm manager for a while during his transition into the operation. We stayed on at the farm until mid 1947 at which time my father and his brother-in-law, Jimmy Darwin bought Nu-Way Laundry and Cleaners in Pulaski. It was over.

The early reports of the sale of the farm said that Albert Noe was going to operate the farm as a dude ranch. Mr. Noe was a chain hotel operator for Jackson, Tennessee. It was later stated that Mr.

Noe was going to operate the farm on a practical basis providing food for the Noe hotels in Jackson, Chattanooga, Birmingham, Alabama, Owensboro, Kentucky and Hopkinsville, Kentucky from its herds of beef and dairy cattle, its poultry, hogs and truck gardens. There was no immediate change of personnel at the farm. After the sale of the farm was announced Life magazine, at that time, Americas most popular pictorial magazine was expected to carry a full picture article of the farm. That type of exposure was expected to bring people from all over the United States to Giles County.

At this time there was a great deal of confusion about exactly what was going to take place in this transition. Everyone was on edge and nervous. After all, the unthinkable had happened. Milky Way Farms had been sold. The employees were disappointed, the community was disappointed and you can bet that Sam Collins was disappointed. Cattle had been moved to Arizona, furniture had been moved from the clubhouse, horses had been sold and the normal stability of the farm was upset.

CHARTER 4-5521

MARS AND HUZENLAUB
2001 NANCE STREET
HOUSTON 10, TEXAS

March 8, 1945

AIRMAIL

Mr. Sam Collins
Milky Way Farm
Pulaski, Tennessee

Dear Sam:

      I had a letter from Abraham saying he wanted to talk to me when I am next at the Farm, so I have dropped him a note that I plan to stp by for a couple of days on my way back from New York and I asked him to talk to you and see if he could not arrange to meet me at the train.

      This is the schedule -- Leave New York via Pennsylvania Pan-American on Saturday, April 7th, at 4:45 P.M., arrive Nashville via L & N 3:43 P.M. April 8th; and I shall be leaving from Nashville for home at 3:55 P.M. on Tuesday the 10th.

      I trust you are all fine, and I shall look forward to seeing you,

             Sincerely,

FEM:jd

Abraham was important enough to the Mars family that Forrest Mars would take time to talk to him.

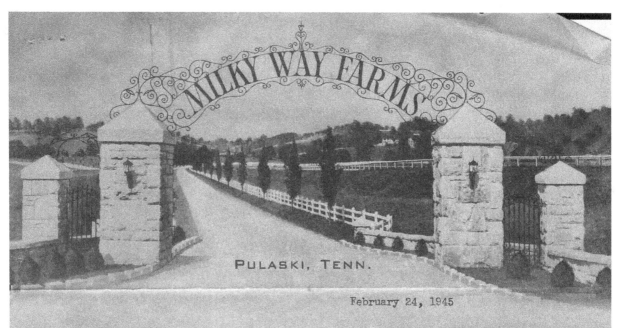

PULASKI, TENN.

February 24, 1945

Mr. Sam Collins
Milky Way Farms
Pulaski, Tenn.

Dear Sam:

Thanks very much for sending me Mrs. Rhea's letter. I heard through Alan that Mr. Rhea was in bad shape and I am afraid that he is not going to pull out of this illness.

Regarding Vernel - do nothing whatever about her bonus, but you might write to her that no one will be paid a bonus until the Farm is sold and at that time her's can be paid. I have been wondering how you are making it on account of Pete and Ed McNeise. I thought there might be some dissatisfaction from the others, because of them receiving their bonus. I hope not.

Alan told me what you said about a good many of the employees laying down on the job and I told him that when he went back to let a few of them go. It is a mean trick to loaf and just lay around with the idea of getting a bonus. I think Alan intends to go back sometime this month.

I am sorry you had such a terrific flood. I can never remember the water being that high before. Hope it is starting to recede. Let me know what damage has been done and how things are going. It has been wise for you to keep in such close touch with Alan and I think he will help you straighten things out when he gets down there. It has been a tough job for you Sam, I know.

I hope Neely is working out satisfactorily. Mrs. Fleming says she enjoys having him at the clubhouse. We are all fine and the weather is lovely.

With kindest regards,

Ethel V. Mars

ETHEL V. MARS

HOME OF REGISTERED HEREFORD CATTLE - THOROUGHBRED HORSES

EVM:Q

Mrs. Mars was worried that some of the employees that she trusted were not carrying through with their part of the bargain. Remember that the severance was contingent on their continuing to work.

Dor mr Sam

I want to no what about my Bones do I got it or are not by mrs mors have turn me over to mrs Jelly I want to no she say she nedd me bad then she did so that i the Reason I on here she say she want me to live with mrs Jelly so I am going to make this my home so do I ask her for one you I thought I would ask you for you are the one that told me about it so Mr Sam Wilie you plaese let me no before mrs mors go for she dont want me to walk out thare any more she told me to stay with mrs Jelly so Wilie you let me no Reasoin plese

so I am still look from Venell to mr Sam tick me to come for it I worked come plese let me no I mrs mors told so I stil look for it

This letter from Vernell Morris to Sam Collins shows the concern about what was taking place at the end of the operation of the farm.

April 2,1945

Mrs.Ethel V.Mars
R#7 Box 466
Phoenix,Arizona

My Dear Mrs.Mars:

Please pardon my delay in not answering your letter sooner
but I have been quite busy and have just neglected same.
I am very sorry that this occured.

I suppose that Alan's cattle have arrived and I surely hope
that they came through in good condition and that none of
them were crippled.I imagine that Alan has arrived back
home and I know he must be enjoying those good cattle.I sure
wish I could see his Ranches because I know they must be
wonderful by the way he talks to me about them.

Well I have really been busy around here for the past few
weeks with showing the prospects and the sale of the farm.
I think that a good sale was made considering everything
but I have never hated to see anything happen so bad in all
my life because it seems to me that I have lost one of the
nicest homes and places to live that I will ever have and
the place will never seem the same to me anymore.I sure hated
to lose the opportunity of getting the place across the road
but I am sure that the sale could not have been made without
 letting the place go with the deal but I sure would have
 liked to have had it.Although I feel that I will be
 taken care of allright in the end and I want you to
 know that I will work for your interest and protect
 your intrest as long as I am in your employ and I

am doing that just now. And will continue to do it until I get my last pay check. I am quite sure that Alan has told you about all the people that have been around and all the goings on that have been happening since the farm was sold. We are taking care of things in as good a manner as possible.

I understood from Mr.Hoben that the bonuses had not yet been approved for the employees. I sure do hope that they are able to get them approved before the delivery date of the farm to Mr.Noe because it is sure going to be bad to have to tell the fellows that their bonuses have not been approved and can't be paid as was promised them when the farm was turned over to the new owner. I talked with Alan about this and I am quite sure that he has discussed it with you and if you can help them to get it approved it sure would be fine, as all the people here are counting on getting the bonus at the time the farm is delivered to the new owner. They will be a badly disappointed group of people, knowing that Pete and Ed and Henry have already received theirs and them not being able to get what was promised them. However, I know that something can be worked out and I know that every effort will be made to work it out by delivery date of the farm.

What do you want done about the bonus of Vernell and Lizzie. Kindly advise me, as to your wishes on their case.

Sure hope that you are feeling better.Alan told me that you had notvbeen feeling so well.I am just fine and have been too busy to feel otherwise.Christine is expecting anytime now and I sure hope that it is a boy.Carolyn is fine and growing like a little pig.

Was in town tonight to see Mr.Rhea.He came back today from Paris and will be at his home in Pulaski.He is much improved and able to be up in the room.However,he looks bad and I am of the opinion that he will not be able to do anything anytime soon.He sure had a close call.He asked about you and all the family.

Give my kindest regards to Marie.

With kindest personal regards,I am

                              Sincerely,

P.S.Neely has worked out fine and has been some good help
    to me.I was just wondering what you thought about
    giving him a bonus.I think it would be nice to give
    him the bonus that Joe Mayfield would have received
    if he had stayed with us.Kindly advise your idea on
    this.

You can tell by the tone of this letter that Sam Collins was worried about the severance pay for the long time employees. The farm had sold to Albert Noe but the deeds had not been signed yet.

FLORIDA BROTHERS & COMPANY

INVESTMENT SECURITIES

MORTGAGE LOANS

OSCEOLA, ARKANSAS

May 7th, 1945.

Mr. Sam Collins,
Milky Way Farms,
Pulaski,
Tenn.

Dear Mr. Collins:

Mr. Noe tells me that some real estate lady in
Evanston, Ill., had a man from New York by the name of
Tiernan who was interested in buying the Milky Way
Farm. I have a friend who owns a nice estate in Virginia
and perhaps Mr. Tiernan would be interested in the Virginia
place, and if you will give me the name of the real estate
lady I will write her.

Thanking you, I am

Yours very truly,

Thos. P. Florida

TPF/s

When you had something for sale that was the magnitude of Milky Way Farms people in high places got the word of who might be a prospective buyer. If you sent a buyer the way of an agent you could get part of a commission.

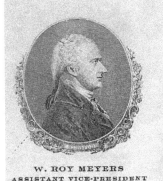

W. ROY MEYERS
ASSISTANT VICE-PRESIDENT

HAMILTON NATIONAL BANK

CHATTANOOGA, TENNESSEE

May 22, 1945

Mr. S. T. Collins, Jr.
Albert Noe Farms
Pulaski, Tennessee

Dear Mr. Collins:

As requested in your letter of May
20th, we are pleased to enclose herewith, a pad of
duplicate deposit tickets and a supply of envelopes
for your use in making your deposits with us by mail.

We also enclose an endorsement stamp
for your use.

Assuring you of our appreciation of
the business with which you are favoring us, and with
kindest regards, we are

Very truly yours,

W. ROY MEYERS
Assistant Vice President

WRM:mhs

Sam Collins was employed by Albert Noe to manage the Albert Noe Farms until Mr. Noe got his arms wrapped around this operation. I included this letter to show the transition from Milky Way Farms to

Albert Noe Farms. My father would say in a correspondence that he didn't believe that the new owner knew what he had on his hands.

MARS *Incorporated*

2019 to 2059 North Oak Park Ave.
Chicago 35, Illinois
May 28, 1945

Mr. S. T. Collins
Albert D. Noe Farms
Pulaski, Tennessee

Dear Sam:

Just a note to tell you that when Mrs. Mars was in the office the other day I mentioned that you would be up here soon. She said to tell you that you would be welcome to stay at her home during the time you are in Chicago.

Until we see you then, best regards.

Yours very truly,

H. H. Hoben
General Manager

HHH/bt

"When you crave good candy — Milky Way"

The farm was sold, the deal was done but Sam Collins still had work to do for both Mars Inc. and for his new employer. Mrs. Mars invited him to stay at her home while he was there to close the final details. He had truly been there from the beginning until the end and after.

Pulaski,Tenn.

June 16,1945

Mr.C.R.Brandon
Credit Manager
Mars Inc.
2019 N.Oak Park Ave.
Chicago,35,Illinois

Dear Mr.Brandon:

I am returning herewith your letter of June 12th to Mr.Noe
regarding the shipment of candy each month,You will note
that it has been okayed by M.Cohen & Sons and Mr.Noe would
appreciate it if you would have the candy shipped assorted,
a few boxes of each kind that you make.

Mr.Brandon,we want you to know that this courtesy is appreciated
very much both by Mr.Noe and myself.

I certainly enjoyed seeing you and visiting with you while in
Chicago recently and if you are near Pulaski at any future time
I want to extend you and invitation to come and visit with me.
Just call me and I will be glad to come and meet you anyplace
that you wish me too.

With kindest personal regards,I am

                              Yours Very Truly,

                              S.T.Collins Jr.

It is interesting to note that part of the deal on the sale of the farm was Mars Inc. would send the new owner of the farm candy each month. M. Cohen & Sons was a wholesaler of grocery goods in Pulaski.

SAME LETTER TO ALBERT III, NEW SOUTHER, JACKSON

July 2, 1945

Mr. Newton Hall,
Dixie Carlton Hotel,
Birmingham, Alabama.

Dear Mr. Hall:

Would you please advise us if you have in the hotel an old kitchen sink which would be suitable for dressing and cleaning chickens.

Thanking you, I am

Very truly yours,

SAM T. COLLINS, Jr.
Farm Manager

STC:hfr

This letter reinforces the plan that Milky Way Farms was going to be converted to raise food stuffs for Mr. Noe's hotel kitchens. Please note that now that Sam Collins is the farm manager for Albert Noe Farms he has a secretary to type his correspondence. That is a step up from his position at Milky Way Farms.

The New Southern

·JACKSON·
TENNESSEE
"AN ALBERT NOE HOTEL"

July 3, 1945

Mr. Sam T. Collins, Jr.
The Albert Noe Farms
Formerly Milky Way Farms
Pulaski, Tennessee

Dear Sam:

Giving you a report on noon, second day,
regarding the Mother and Nora Noe's condition. They
are both fine and doing as well as can be expected.
I think Mary Happel's progress is because of her
happiness in having a daughter. We are all very pleased
and especially the grandparents.

I am instructing Mr. Moore at the Owensboro
to ship you the three sinks we have at Owensboro with the
proper fittings for same. They will be coming by truck.

All of my family including Nora join me in
sending kindest regards to you and your family.

Cordially yours,

Albert

N:E   Albert

THE DIXIE CARLTON
BIRMINGHAM, ALA.

THE OWENSBORO
OWENSBORO, KY.

Albert Noe Hotels are Hotels of Distinction

THE READ HOUSE
CHATTANOOGA, TENN.

This letter had a twofold purpose. It announced the arrival of Albert Noe's daughter and the fact that the sinks that had been requested were being shipped from the Owensboro. Take note of the inside address and how it explains the new name and the former name.

Pulaski,Tennessee

July 4,1945

Mrs.Ethel V.Mars
930 Ashland Ave.
River Forest,Illinois

My Dear Mrs.Mars:

How are you feeling by now?Surely do hope that you are much
improved.I have intended writing you sooner but have been quite
busy since I returned home.

I was not able to get the Bottling Works deal thru.Mr.Smith and
I have spent quite a bit of time and thought on it and would have
taken it but just couldn't find anyplace to move the plant or
anyplace we could lease temporarily,and when it came down to the
showdown the fellow that wanted to sell wouldn't let us use his
building any longer than the first of this coming year.So after
much work and thought we had to let it pass because we just
couldn't see as much money as we would have to put out for the
franchise and equipment and after the first of the year would have
no place to do business.I have another thing or two working now
and just don't know how long it will take for them to work out.
However,I am trying my best to work out some kind of business
that looks good to me and will let you know if I line up anything.

Mrs.Mars,I wonder if it would be asking too much of you or whether
it would be in order to ask you to give me a recommendation now or
would it be better to wait until I am off the payroll which you
know will be about four years from now.I don't need the recommendation now but might need one at some future time.I would appreiate
your suggestion and idea on it. Mrs.Mars,again I want to thank
you from the bottom of my heat for the many courtesies shown me
while there and for the nice time that I spent with you in your
home.Also for the wonderful manner in which you took care of me
in the closing out of the farm deal.You will never know what it
will mean to me and I will try and always keep the money invested
in something that will be a living monument to the grandest boss
one ever had and the grandest woman that I have ever known.Again
I want to thank you and at the end of the four year period in which
it was agreed that I would draw the money I hope to have it invested
in something that I can write you and tell you again what it means
to me and just how much you have helped me get a start.

Abraham hasn't been well since he came back from Phoenix and has
just been dragging around here.He dosen't know what to do with
himself or his time.He talks like he wants to work at some light
work around here to keep his mind occupied.He also said that he
was planning on coming up to see you sometime this summer.

We have really been having some hot weather down here. The farm looks very well and have been putting up lots of hay.

The people just can't seem to realize what they have bought. They are absolutely lost and I am begining to wonder if it isn't too big a thing for them to handle. Sure dosen't seem anything near the same place and I am getting awfully anxious to get something lined up for myself and will letvyou know as soon as I do get anything.

How is Marie getting along? Give her my regards. How is Mrs. Feeney and Alan andthe children. Haven't heard from them in some time.

Christine and the children are just doing fine. Christine is about to work herself to death with two children to care for and we just can't get any help at all. The baby sure is growing fast.

Surely do hope that you are much improved and with kindest personal regards, I am

Sincerely,

This is the last letter from my father to Mrs. Mars. You have noticed that in any letter my father always inquired about her health. Her health was failing rapidly. If you remember the situation about the bonuses and that my father had asked for a $10,000.00 bonus for himself and that had been reduced by $6,000.00 and change, you also remember that I said that he would latter receive the entire amount. Well, Albert Noe wanted my father to stay with him as the farm manager until he got his feet on the ground. My father agreed to do so if he were given the rest of the bonus that he had recommended himself for. This was worked out and was to be paid over a four year period. I told you that he would get the rest of his severance and he did. This letter emphasizes that my father doesn't believe that Albert Noe had any idea what he had bought. He also didn't believe that they could handle the operation that they intended to install. My father wanted to serve his allotted time with Albert Noe Farms and as soon as possible find a business to operate. That business would be Nu-Way Laundry and Cleaners in Pulaski with his brother in law, Jimmy Darwin.

ALBERT NOE FARMS

NOE BETTER HEREFORDS

October 17, 1945 — OUR FIRST HEREFORD AUCTION — Pulaski, Tenn.

The Milky Way Farms logo on the catalog had been changed to Albert Noe Farms.

In mid-July of 1945 the Noe plans for the farm were taking place. The plans for a dude ranch were fading fast and the conversion of the farm to a producer of food for his hotels and the nation were taking place. The first step in that direction was to convert the 487 foot horse barn into a chicken barn.

Tennessee's Largest Broiler Plant Housing 20,000 Chickens Produced With Special Care for the Albert Noe Hotels.

A Royal Welcome, Always, at the Hotels and the Farms

THE NEW SOUTHERN
JACKSON, TENN.

THE OWENSBORO
OWENSBORO, KY.

THE READ HOUSE
CHATTANOOGA, TENN.

THE DIXIE CARLTON
BIRMINGHAM, ALA.

The ALBERT NOE HOTELS are Hotels of Distinction

McCOWAT-MERCER, JACKSON, TENN.

This advertisement was on the back of the catalog that was shown on the last page. A truly diehard Milky Way Farms lover could hardly look at this advertisement without true disdain. It was truly over, indeed.

His goal was to produce five hundred frying size chickens a day. A dressing and quick freezing plant was installed and seven thousand chicks were brought to the Noe Farms. The dressing and quick freezing plant were of great interest to everyone since that would allow for immediate delivery to any of the six hotels in his hotel empire. Two thousand chicks were expected to be added each week until a total of twenty two thousand two hundred would be in production. Some folks who recall the history of the farm tend to believe that Milky Way Farms was in the production of walking horses. That mistaken idea comes from the fact that Albert Noe was a walking horse enthusiast and believed that the addition of walking horses would be a good thing since they were becoming very popular in the mid-state. He was into whatever would make money.

Since I am trying to do this in almost chronological order this is a good place to put this photo. My sister and I in our yard at the farm. I'm the good looking one without much hair.

Albert Noe was not a new comer to the cattle business. He had a large herd on his Jackson, Tennessee estate. When he bought the farm he also bought the Hereford cattle that Alan Feeney had not carried to Arizona with him. On October 17, 1945 Mr. Noe advertised an auction that would include forty females and ten bulls that were in the stock that he got when he bought the farm. By offering these "Milky Way Farms" cattle it might make him a legitimate top notch breeder and give him nationwide notoriety. The sale was advertised on a national scale. Col. Art Thompson of Lincoln, Nebraska was in charge of the sale and had correspondence from California to Florida about the upcoming event. The local Exchange Club would be in charge of the food. The barbecue meal would be prepared from "Noe" Herefords along with the usual sides and desserts served by the Exchange members and their wives. One of the first nationally recognized walking horse sales, the J.J. Murray sale in Lewisburg, Tennessee, would be held in that same two day span. Since Mr. Noe was a walking horse enthusiast he thought that having his sale at the same time would bring a large crowd to the mid-state and have a positive effect on both parties. If you are a local walking horse enthusiast you will remember that the Murray Farm sale in Lewisburg was a sale that attracted many future champions and people from all over the United States attended this two day event. Two local men, Pete Yokley and Sam Yarborough, were instrumental in the success of this sale. In September, 1947 "Noe News" won the pony class at the Tennessee Walking Horse Celebration in Shelbyville. A local young man exhibited this horse for the Noe Stables. J.D. Coffman III, young son of Mr. and Mrs. J.D. Coffman Jr. of Pulaski who had established a name for himself as an exhibitor and rider of winning horses in shows of this section of the country won the pony class for the Noe Farms. As manager of the "Noe Hereford Farm" my father publicized this sale and received inquiries from twenty-eight states and Canada. He used the fact that Mr. Noe had just bought the highest priced Hereford bull that had ever been purchased by a Tennessean and brought it to the farm. This bull was Baca R. Domino 33rd that he purchased in Crestone, Colorado for $27,700. Mr. Noe's opening remarks included high praise for Ralph Freeman, Alan Feeney and Brown Hardiman for their handling of the famous Milky Way Farms cattle.

The people of Giles County were sad to learn that Mrs. Ethel V. Mars had died at noon on Christmas day of 1945 in a hospital at La Jolla, California. A requiem mass was sung at La Jolla, on the following Friday morning at St. Mary's Star of the Saint Church with entombment at a later date at Lakewood Cemetery, Minneapolis Minnesota.

WESTERN UNION

A. N. WILLIAMS
PRESIDENT

NHR1 NL PD= SANDIEGO CALIF 25
SAM COLLINS=
PULASKI, TENN.

MOTHER SUDDENLY PASSED AWAY AT NOON TODAY ROSARY THURSDAY
EVENING BONHAM MORTUARY SAN DIEGO MASS FRIDAY MORNING AT
ST MARYS STAR OF THE SEAS LAJOLLA. INTERMENT LAKEWOOD
MINNEAPOLIS LATER=

PATRICIA MARS FEENEY.

This is the telegram that Sam Collins received to inform him of the death of Mrs. Mars.

Interment will take place in
June, Nineteen Forty-Six
Lakewood Cemetery
Minneapolis, Minnesota

NOTICE OF EXACT DATE LATER

This card came later to let everyone know that her interment would take place in June of 1946.

Services and interment
for the late Ethel V. Mars
will be conducted by the Rev. M. L. Doyle
on Saturday, June 1, 1946, at 10:00 a.m.
in the chapel at Lakewood Cemetery
3600 Hennepin Avenue
Minneapolis, Minnesota

The exact date of Mrs. Mar's services and interment would be June 1, 1946 at Lakewood Cemetery in Minneapolis, Minnesota.

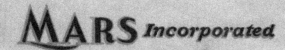

MARS *Incorporated*

2019 to 2059 North Oak Park Ave.
Chicago 35, Illinois
January 7, 1946

Mr. Sam T. Collins, Jr.
% Albert Noe Farms
Pulaski, Tenn.

Dear Sam:

I want to thank you for your letter of January 6.

The passing of Mrs. Mars was somewhat of a shock; however, we expected it to happen but hoped that she would hang on for another few years. As you no doubt know, she was not well for quite a period of time. In fact, last summer she spent three fourths of the time in bed up at the lake.

She went to Phoenix this fall and stood the trip fairly well. As it was Patty's intention to be in California for Christmas, she decided to make the trip over to be with her. According to Patty, she arrived four or five days before Christmas by plane and apparently was feeling quite well. She continued to feel well until noon the day before Christmas at which time she took a turn for the worse. About midnight, Patty rushed her to the hospital, and although she showed signs of recovering two or three times during the night, it seemed it was just out of the question for her to make it and she passed away about noon Christmas Day.

The internment at Lakewood Cemetery in Minneapolis will be some time the early part of June. We intend to send out notices as to the definite date later on.

Patty expects to be here at 930 Ashland Avenue, River Forest, within the next week or ten days, so if you care to write her she can be reached there.

Hoping that you and your family have all recovered from the flu, I am

Yours Sincerely,

WLK/ah   MARS, INCORPORATED

By: *W. L. Kruppenbacher*
W.D. Kruppenbacher
Chairman of the Board of Directors & President

"When you crave good candy — Milky Way"

This letter gives the details of Mrs. Mars' last days.

Mrs. Mars was in ill health for about four years but her death was unexpected at the time it occurred. She had been residing in River Forrest, Illinois and was visiting her daughter, Mrs. Alan Feeney of Phoenix, Arizona when she died. She and her husband were remembered for the hope that they gave Giles County during the early days of the depression. Giles County labor was used to clear, hand-rake, landscape, paint buildings and fences and carpenter labor for the many buildings on the farm. After the death of her husband in keeping with their interest in the progress of the community, she made a contribution of several thousand dollars for the erection of the Catholic Church located on south First Street. This was done in memory of her husband, she was a Catholic. A further donation of several hundred dollars was make to the Presbyterian Church near the farm, her husband was a Presbyterian. As has been previously stated Mr. Mars favored saddle horses and Mrs. Mars liked race horses. In horse circles she was obviously remembered for owning the 1940 winner of the Kentucky Derby, Gallahadion. Not as well publicized was the fact that her horses shared in the Derby purse twice previously with Whiskolo and Reaping Reward finishing third in 1935 and 1937 respectively.

In 1934 and 1936 Milky Way Farms Stables was the turf's leading money winner. Mrs. Mars was born in Grafton, North Dakota, June 25, 1884 and spent her early life in Minnesota where she met and married Franklin C. Mars. She worked with her husband to build a modest candy company in Tacoma, Washington into a corporate giant. Her obituary listed her survivors as: one daughter, Patricia Mars Feeney, several grandchildren and one brother, William L. Kruppenbacher of Chicago.

When Mrs. Mars will was probated it showed her estate was worth $275,000.00. Under the terms of the document on file in the probate court of Cook County, Illinois $11,000.00 was bequeathed to four servants and the balance was left in trust to her daughter, Mrs. Alan Feeney and to Mrs. Feeney's six children.

If you continue to look at the history of Milky Way Farms you will soon see that Milky Way Farms is not friendly to men who take ownership of this piece of property. Mr. Mars died three years into his ownership and on September 27, 1947 Albert Noe Jr. died of a heart attack at a Memphis Hospital. Funeral services were held at 11:00 a.m. at the First Presbyterian Church in Jackson, Tennessee. He was fifty-eight years of age. He had owned the farm scarcely over two years. Albert Noe III vowed to continue his father's work at the farm. He held a Hereford sale at the farm on November 11, 1947 to show the public that he would indeed continue his father's work and love for cattle. What was now called Albert Noe Farms was used in June of 1948 as the backdrop for scenes in a walking horse movie that depicted the history of the walking horse in the state of Tennessee. Local personalities were used in the film. Will Shaw, farmer and breeder of the Diana community; Bobby Harwell, high school student from Pulaski; John Taylor from Allisonia; and Myrom Wolaver; horseman and farmer of the Diana Community were used in the film. This $20,000 film was produced for the Tennessee Walking Horse Association. There are many in Giles County that believe that the Milky Way Farms of Mars fame had Tennessee walking horses. What I just described about the Noe fascination with walking horses is where that misconception came from.

After his father's death in late 1947 Albert Noe III made every attempt possible to assure everyone that he would continue his father's work and maintain the farm.

This dispersal sale was held November 11th and 12th of 1949. Everybody should have known that it was over.

However, in July 1950 he sold the farm to four Lewisburg business men. They were E.K. Harwell, Hereford breeder and owner of Lazy Valley farms near Lewisburg; J. Lee Moss, president of First National Bank of Lewisburg; R.L. McBride Jr., vice president of the First National Bank of Lewisburg and Ernest Henegar, partner in the Marshall County Creamery at Lewisburg and brother of Harold Henegar of Pulaski who was the owner of the Giles County Dairy Products Company. No sale price was made known but an unofficial figure was set at approximately $500,000. Though the plans for the operation of the farm were indefinite most people thought that it would be some type of livestock operation. The Pulaski Citizen in October, 1950 ran an article that was supposed to dispel rumors in the community that the four new owners were considering selling the farm off in smaller tracts. In November, 1950 one of the original four purchasers of the farm sold his interest to the other three partners. Ladies and gentlemen, IT WAS OVER. From this point the farm that brought worldwide fame to Giles County was cut up into smaller tracts and its demise began. Earlier in our discussion I told you that in the 1950's when we would go north on highway 31 my mother couldn't bear to see the once famous prize of Giles County in disarray and would look the other way or just close her eyes. The best years of their lives were spent at Milky Way Farms.

In the last paragraph I said that in 1950 it was over. By that I meant that the breakup of the farm had begun. We have looked at Milky Way Farms from its inception in 1930 to 1950. In no way would the breakup of the farm into smaller tracts erase the memory of Milky Way Farms from those who loved her. I know that the farm will never be put back exactly like it was, that is impossible. The people that own parts of her now will always be able to say that they live on something that is so dear to many in Giles County. She was dear to so many during such desperate times and will remain dear to those who keep the original memory alive. I am thankful that there are members of our community like the present owners that are striving to keep the dream and memory alive.

Sam T. Collins Jr. sitting at his desk in the office at Milky Way Farm after he was named the Resident Agent for Mars Incorporated.

On the last page you saw a photo of my father sitting at his desk in the office at Milky Way Farms. This typewriter is the one that all of his correspondence was typed on. This typewriter can be seen behind his left shoulder. I have this typewriter and all the other information and documents in this book in the material that my father left to me. I didn't put all the information that I have in this book because it would be too large and cumbersome. I want to thank God for the opportunity of sharing some of the history of Milky Way Farms with you. God bless you and Semper fi.

Appendix:

The photos in this appendix are in no particular order. They are presented here to give the reader a look into the daily operation, activities and buildings on the farm.

These mules and their show harness were used on a daily basis.

These teams were used to help build the race track.

Mules were used on a daily basis.

Notice the riding britches. Mr. Mars bought several of these jackets for his own use and for others.

The three musketeers behind the office.

Notice the barn behind this colt.

Beautiful colts like this were commonplace at the farm. Notice the barn in the background.

Unloading Horned Hereford cattle.

Notice the sheep barns on top of the hill.

These barns were unique to Milky Way Farms.

Patty and Alan at the gardens.

I was getting weighed in a unique scale that was usually used in a store.

The car would be a real collector today.

This was one of the more famous gaited studs.

Notice the sheep barn in the middle of the photo.

Fed cattle were an important part of the farm's operation.

Elevated view of the feeder barns.

This photo was taken at the mule barn.

Horse barn.

Feeder barns.

Milky Way Farms had a fleet of these trucks.

Sheep made up an important part of the livestock operation.

These fed cattle would make their way to Chicago.

All of these feed lot cattle were not raised on the farm.

Each handler was very proud of their team.

What a beautiful view of the Milky Way Farms rolling hills.

Horned Hereford cows in the breeding pen.

This colt seemed ready for a new world.

Milky Way Farms had several prize studs.

Young mules had to learn what was expected of them.

Prize road horse stud.

Five gaited horse breaking on the rail.

Handsome colts ruled the day in the early years at Milky Way Farms.

A road horse on the rail.

The racetrack in its early formative stage.

I know that you have seen this photo before. Go to the next page and see if you see anything in that photo that you don't notice in this one.

On page 259 that photo did not have the lower barn in it. This photo was obviously taken later.

Grey Mare Mules-Beck and Lize

Registered Hereford barn.

Please look at this photo carefully. When most people look at it they are excited because they believe this has got to be the first clubhouse. It is not. This house was located on the spot where Roger Reedy and his wife live now. This house was destroyed by fire but it was in ill repair for a long time. When the first clubhouse burned this house was used by Mr. and Mrs. Mars when they were at the farm. If you look closely when you go north on highway 31 you will see the circular drive and the rock posts at the end of the drive. This house was located right before the Richland Creek Bridge.

The house in the Wildwoods.

A worker putting insulation in the new clubhouse.

Putting up hay in the center of the racetrack.

Horned Hereford cattle grazed the hillsides at Milky Way Farms.

The view from the location where the mausoleum would be built.

The subfloor and insulation in the new clubhouse.

Holstein cattle around one of the many springs on the farm. The abundance of fresh water was very beneficial to all the livestock operations.

Notice that these cattle at the Chicago stockyard were fed by Milky Way Farms but were bred in Colorado.

This view of the clubhouse shows the walk to the front door and the type of shrubbery used at that time.

Another view of the construction of the racetrack.

James Drake's sheep barn that went around the hill made the news and the Guinness Book of Records.

Purebred Hereford Barn.

Race Horse Barn.

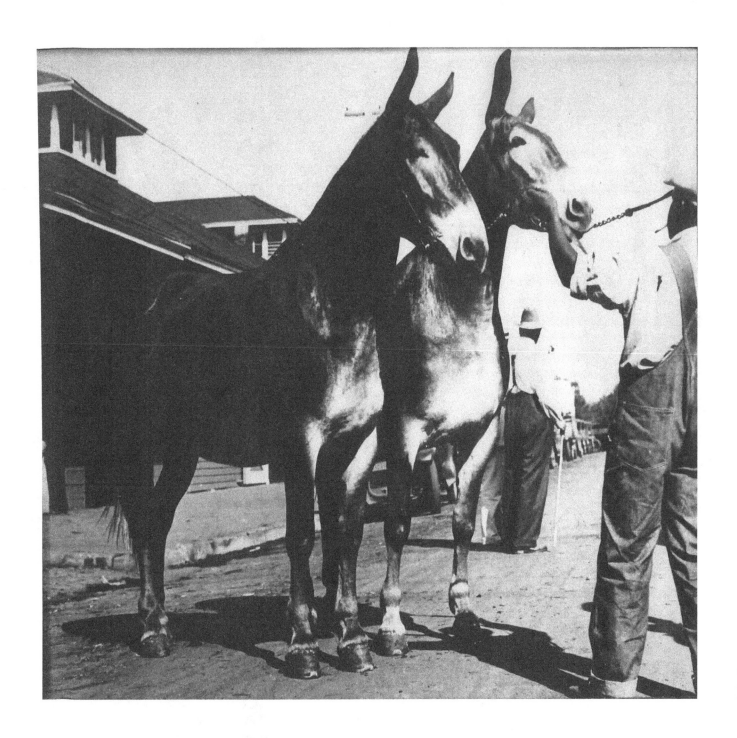

Sorrell horse and mare mules-Jake and Kate.

CPSIA information can be obtained
at www.ICGtesting.com
Printed in the USA
JSHW051744210523
41928JS00002B/6

9 780692 267202